D1473705

Help
Your Boss
&
Help
Yourself

DRAWINGS BY HENRY MARTIN

Help Your Boss & Help Yourself

*

Nathaniel Stewart

Fairleigh Dickinson
University Library

Teaneck, New Jersey

amacom
A DIVISION OF AMERICAN MANAGEMENT ASSOCIATIONS

International standard book number: 0-8144-5351-1
Library of Congress catalog card number: 73-87547
First printing

to
Raymond L. Randall
manager, educator, and devoted friend

PREFACE

Contrary to popular belief, many bosses do not have ulcers —but they are carriers. Your boss may be one of the carriers. You can see it coming in the day-to-day tensions, blunders, tantrums, disappointments, and flare-ups at the workplace. For Joan, it is the office locale; for Hank, the warehouse. For others, it is the shop, the department, the plant, the division headquarters, the shift, or the sales district. Each of them "catches" it.

One man who had been working in such an environment for some time told a consultant who interviewed him: "I'll level with you and put it this way: they say there's heart in this company; yeah, working for this boss there's heartache, heartburn, and heart failure!" There was a very audible "Amen" from his co-workers.

In many cases you should feel truly sorry for this boss, for he is caught in a syndrome. He would like to perform as a pro and measure up to the standards of a good manager. At the same time, he is victimized by his self-image, limitations, emotions, and biases. He is trapped by outside incidents and influences. These counteract his desire to behave and perform effectively as a manager. Unable to make it, he is subjected to criticism, bypassed, threatened, or otherwise made uncomfortable by his superiors or his peers. Life for him is not easy.

At the same time, you should feel sorry for yourself. As his subordinate, you too are caught in a syndrome. On the one hand, you feel that your boss ought to stand or fall on his own merit, and that it is not your responsibility to prop him up. If he doesn't have what it takes to perform as a manager, the company ought to get rid of him. (But companies do not get rid of or displace bosses as readily as all that.) On the other hand, as long as he remains limited, erratic, or mismatched in his assignment, life on the job with him will be difficult, strained, and discouraging. You wish there was something you could do to help. In essence, you wish you could improve the situation for your own well-being, your physical and emotional health, and your desire to work in a compatible, productive climate. Life for you too is not easy.

The boss has his pressures and frustrations, and he releases them on you and others in the department. What's his hangup? Very often it is this: he is not measuring up to what his boss expects of him in the way of performance, he is not fulfilling his own aims and aspirations, or both. He is regarded as just a mediocre, tolerable, marginal manager. As is often stated in the business world, he's not good enough to be promoted or poor enough to be fired.

In many companies the pattern is the same: one mistake and this boss gets the isolation treatment; two mistakes and he is bypassed for any kind of recognition or prospects; three mistakes and he is written off as a has-been.

Whether he has made one, two, or three mistakes, this boss gets into a rut. He becomes edgy and overcautious, reluctant to express his ideas for fear of being rejected. He feels threatened by a new announcement or the arrival of a new man. All this adds up to tension and emotional pressure. As a result, he continually criticizes you and others, engages in nitpicking and pettiness, and resorts to outbursts and threats. He loses his zest for the job and begins to daydream, play it safe, and work at only routine tasks. All these are expressions of his built-up tension and insecurity.

Now, there may not even be much wrong with this boss. In most cases, he is not a misfit, an emotional cripple, or an incompetent. He can be charged only with being mediocre, with having limited competency, or with having gone stale. Something can be done about it. After all, he did have something on the ball at one time and it may be that he still does. It is possible to help this boss perform more effectively as a manager. That is the essence of this book. It is concerned with what the boss can do, what you can do, and what you and he can do together to make life on the job more productive and rewarding.

It takes some kind of catalyst to energize him and get him out of his rut. You, the subordinate, can be that catalyst. You can help your boss look good to his own boss. Indeed, you may even be able to help him save his job. It may also be the pathway to your own progress and success on the job. It can be done.

Just what can you do to help your boss overcome his limitations and perform more effectively? How can you do it? Why should you do it? Are there different types of bosses who need your help? Do they have different kinds of blindspots that hold them back? And are they to be managed differently? Read on—and see.

Nathaniel Stewart

CONTENTS

YOUR BOSS MAY BE SLIPPING

Your boss may be slipping. The slippage may be slow and cumulative, or it may have come to light only recently and rather suddenly, surprising you and others in the department.

Symptoms of Slippage

For the most part, evidence of slippage is to be found in how your boss performs in everyday management practice. Here are some of the bits of evidence. He fails to take advantage of a good opportunity; he is not well prepared for an important meeting; he is plagued with deadlines and throws the department into a panic trying to meet them. Or he is slow about getting to rather urgent items in his in-basket; he allows grievances to go unresolved; he looks upon reports as just so much routine and nonsense; he shrugs off top management announcements of new policies as of little consequence but cautions his people to follow them anyway. Errors or inaccuracies show up in his work — more than usual; proposals or suggestions from subordinates are shelved without explanation; there is slack in his coordination with managers of other departments; he begins to shy away from problems and to defer decisions, whether big or small; he is unresponsive to organizational weaknesses that need troubleshooting. All these give evidence that a manager may be slipping.

Superiors, associates, and subordinates can judge a manager's slippage only in terms of his actions — whether or not he is measuring up to his responsibilities in day-to-day management of the department. You can see these things and judge them objectively. It becomes more difficult and more dangerous to judge slippage in terms of attitudes and reactions. Granted that changes in attitudes manifest themselves along with changes in performance. Your boss may appear to you to be more irritable, suspicious, or cynical than before. He may seem less enthusiastic and more neglectful. He may display that "tired feeling" or show a desire to be alone. Yet it is difficult to make a judgment on such attitudes until they begin to form a clear pattern. So exercise caution in jumping to conclusions.

To repeat, in making your judgment, focus on the incidents, the acts, the evidence that emerges in day-to-day management of the office, the department, or the plant. Afterward, you might be sufficiently observant to note and draw implications relative to attitudinal changes. The reason for this caution: there's more to it than meets the eye, and generally only trained professionals are perceptive enough to identify and link the incidents, the attitudes, and the behavior that spell managerial slippage. Let's see what professionally trained psychologists, psychiatrists, consultants, and others have to say about the manager who is failing to measure up to his responsibilities.

YOUR BOSS MAY BE SLIPPING

One observer points to indicators such as these in spotting whether a boss is slipping:

When he talks more about what he did in the past than what he plans to do in the future.

When he blames failures on conditions, new competition, pressure.

When he begins to lose interest in figures—data on which management judgments often have to be based.

When he begins to believe that the company can't get along without him.

When he becomes adept at finding reasons why a new idea or method won't work.

When he confides to friends that his boss doesn't appreciate the years he has given to the company.

When he gripes that his position rates a bigger office, a bigger staff.

When he arrives later, lunches longer, leaves earlier.

When he loses the knack of talking *with* people and begins to talk *at* them—talking down to suppliers, customers, other managers, secretaries, and so on.

Still another profile of the obsolescent manager is presented by Philip Marvin, a consultant to General Foods, Corning Glass, Johnson & Johnson, and other organizations:

He is inflexible—does not recognize new needs and opportunities; has rigid and stereotyped approaches to assignments; is reliant mainly on past practices.

He is closed to new ideas—resists, stalls, shelves ideas.

He is self-centered—satisfied and complacent with things as he finds them; defends his citadel.

He doesn't make any constructive suggestions.

He assumes a defensive posture.

He is a low-risk man—believes that the best way to avoid mistakes is to do little or nothing.

He lives in the past.

He doesn't know what he wants to do—decisions are governed by expediency, not goals.[1]

Some observers use the term "diaper management" in describing the manager who is slipping. The principle of diaper management is simple: No matter what happens, keep your rear end covered. Diaper managers are those with alibis, excuses, rationalizations. Nothing is quite their fault—it is the fault of the system, the establishment, a subordinate, a secretary. They dispatch memos on why an assignment or a project might fail before they even start on it. This too is a sign of slippage.

In his book *The Managerial Mind,* David Ewing lists some common blinders—contrived techniques—that the obsolescent manager resorts to in order to avoid dealing with obstacles:

Blinder 1: overemphasis on security. He insists on security at all costs. This could be dangerous, for absolute security can be attained only by avoiding risk and change and adhering blindly to the way things were done in the past.

Blinder 2: putting harmony first. He avoids honest controversy and makes a fetish of agreement, thereby obscuring problems in the department.

Blinder 3: substituting routines for thinking. He is overly committed to routine. Some routine is fine, but it can be dangerous if it is used to replace sound thinking.

Blinder 4: schedulitis. He is so preoccupied with agenda that he is unable to listen to or to accommodate new ideas.

Blinder 5: compulsion to show status. He is preoccupied with status symbols. When this pattern begins to dominate, it leads to managerial isolation—from customers, associates, subordinates, and others.

Blinder 6: fetish with orderliness. He is concerned that nothing upset the tidiness of his pet projects. He refuses to do anything unconventional and is afraid to face reality, which may be upsetting.

Blinder 7: obsession with firm conclusions. He makes sweeping generalizations—everything is either right or wrong, hon-

[1] Philip Marvin, *Multiplying Management Effectiveness* (AMA, 1971), pp. 13–15.

est or fraudulent—to evade more rigorous analysis. This black-and-white reasoning often leads to naive and simplistic conclusions. He is unable to recognize problems in the gray areas.[2]

Other observers see managerial slippage, obsolescence, and the onset of "failure" as resulting from the following factors: complacency, satisfaction with present conditions, lack of ability to keep up with organizational pressures and complexity, age factor (in some people) twisted to imply that one is too old to learn, resistance to change, and acceptance of one's present success or affluence as the formula for what will continue forever.

Psychologist Walter Mahler draws more specific lines regarding managerial obsolescence. He views it in terms of different types of obsolescence:

Abrupt obsolescence: when technological innovation, such as the introduction of a new computer system, eliminates the need for or drastically changes a manager's job; this could also happen in the course of a major reorganization.

Creeping obsolescence: when the nature of the job changes slowly and the manager gradually ossifies; he develops a kind of hardening of the arteries.

Pseudo-obsolescence: when the company lays off a large number of managers at one time, for whatever reason.

Abilities obsolescence: when a manager's skills and abilities are no longer sufficient to meet past or current job demands and are totally insufficient to meet new demands.

Attitudinal obsolescence: when a manager fails to maintain the flexibility of attitude and approach that he needs to deal with changing goals, problems, conditions, and relationships.

Industrial obsolescence: when an entire industry becomes obsolescent; this problem is broader than that of any individual manager.[3]

---

[2] David W. Ewing, *The Managerial Mind* (Glencoe, Ill.: Free Press of Glencoe, 1964), p. 65.

[3] Walter Mahler, "Every Company's Problem: Managerial Obsolescence," *Personnel* (July–August 1965), pp. 8–16.

An obsolescent manager—or even one who is slipping considerably—can be defined as a once capable manager who has lost his ability to keep pace with modernization, growth, or change. As a result, he is no longer as effective as he should be. Drawing upon Mahler's delineations, then, we are concerned with skills obsolescence and attitudinal obsolescence of the manager. And something can be done about these.

Physicians and psychiatrists have often indicated that the early manifestations of stress in the manager who is slipping are mental and physical fatigue, difficulty in adjusting to new experiences, resistance to rapidly changing environmental factors, and a feeling of threat to his security and self-esteem. All this could well lead to an unhealthy emotional state on the job—anxiety, fear, anger, withdrawal, conflict.

Psychiatrists also acknowledge that the organizational climate can contribute to managerial decline. Emotional stress can be compounded by too much responsibility, overwork, excessive pressures, lack of clarity as to the real authority of one's position, and conflicting obligations (to one's boss, peers, clients, subordinates, and others) because of role ambiguity. At times, the climate engenders an uncomfortable social role as well. The obsolescent manager is uncomfortable in that he cannot always trust those around him; some will butter him up, others will complain about him, and still others will appear hostile. Thus he experiences very limited friendships in the work setting. The loss of friendship or camaraderie—whether due to his own limitations or to the organizational climate—robs him of an important motivation as a manager of others.

The seriousness of these manifestations and of the impact on the man is the subject of several studies by psychologist Eugene Jennings. Against the background of the Adlerian thesis that one has to make adjustments in the major areas of his life—social adjustment, work adjustment, adjustment to love-marriage-family, and so on—Jennings maintains that adjustment to or success in the occupational area not only is most highly valued in our culture but often preempts all other areas of life. His studies disclose this salient point: "Failure in this one area of life activity [the work setting] cannot be easily compensated for by success in any of the other life areas. . . . In short, over a period of time career and work concern and demands occupy the major share of his life—and life and work tend to become overlapping and synonymous."[4]

This may explain the tension, stress, and maladjustment to the work environment of the manager who is slipping. The need for self-esteem and respectability persists. As William James observed many years ago, one of the deepest cravings of man is the desire to be recognized.

What, then, does the manager who is slipping do? In the more acute cases, when he becomes very sensitive to criticism from his co-workers, he will find some way to counter his own feelings. Psychiatrists suggest this spectrum of possible behaviors in people who attempt to counter their feelings:

Emotional block: being at a loss for words.

Taking flight: talking about other things to displace the real incident; projecting the blame on to some other person or thing.

Hitting back: responding angrily; striking at the aggressor.

Suppression: squelching one's feelings, as if beaten and ready to quit; giving nonverbal expressions of discomfort.

Ambivalence: having difficulty in expressing oneself because one is torn between opposing feelings—the desire to fight back and the desire to avoid conflict.

Moving toward: giving verbal or nonverbal expressions of empathy; wanting to continue the relationship and to get the difference solved.

Laughter: venting one's feelings through a nervous kind of half-laughter rather than directing them at the other party.

You may recognize some of these symptoms in your boss.

Top management uses a variety of techniques to deal with the manager who is slipping. The techniques include easing him out of a key spot, giving him the pink slip, endowing him with a phony

[4] Eugene E. Jennings, *The Executive in Crisis* (East Lansing: Graduate School of Business Administration, Michigan State University, 1965), p. 168.

title (and even kicking him upstairs) with little or no responsibility, lowering the retirement age so as to expedite his departure, transferring him to some corporate dumping ground, redesigning his job so that he winds up with limited activity, and carrying on a cold war with him by encouraging his close friends to tell him he's over the hill. Only in rare instances does top management actually try to retrain or retool him, counsel with him, or redesign his job meaningfully so that he can retain some sense of productiveness and dignity.

Granted there is no chivalry in management. But neither should there be brutality.

Let us examine what the critics have had to say about managerial slippage and what others have done, or professed should be done, to deal with this problem.

The Critics and Their Target

Taking potshots at the marginal manager has become a cultural pastime. Name calling, derogatory remarks, and demeaning references to managers are widespread. Writers and lecturers have had a field day deriding managers, classifying them into types and giving them labels. It has become sporting to get in some digs at managers to enliven an otherwise dull piece of writing or a boring lecture.

Labels like the ones below usually provoke quick recognition of someone you know and then, if humorous details are added, bring a reaction ranging from an amused snicker to a boisterous belly laugh.

the has-been	the godfather
the butter-upper	the let-nature-take-
the flipflop	its-course type
the empire builder	the great indispen-
the politician	sable man
the bulldozer	the blind-leading-
the boat-misser	the-blind type
the hatchet man	the buttinsky

8

the do-nothing

the double bogey

the despot

the manipulator

the plotter

the loser

the bluffer

the hand-sitter

the overspecialist

the secret weapon

the loner

the little man

the bureaucrat

the De Gaullist

the great compromiser

the "nice guy, but . . ."
  manager

the crusader

the do-it-all

the square peg in
  a round hole

the retired-before-
  his-time type

the POPO (passed over,
  put on the shelf)

the hold-it-until-
  next-Tuesday type

the hot-potato-
  passer

the haphazard type

More sophisticated classifiers place managers in the autocratic, democratic, and laissez-faire categories, or in the Theory X and Theory Y patterns, or in the Blake-Mouton Managerial Grid® chart from 1,1 to 9,9 to indicate minimum and maximum concern for people and results.

Let's face it. Some managers do fall into one or another of these slots. You don't have to be a social anthropologist or a clinical psychiatrist to spot them. Every employee has encountered this or that type at some point in his career. *However, the vast majority of marginal or inadequate managers are not so easily classified. Generally, they can only be charged with mediocrity, with having limited competency, with having gone stale.* Moreover, most marginal managers have the potential to rise above their mediocrity, to broaden themselves and their outlook, and to get out of the rut. It takes some kind of catalyst, of course. You, as a subordinate, can play just such a role.

Managers are neither saints nor sinners, neither sages nor fools. They run the gamut of human talents and frailties, as do individuals in all other occupations. Bosses may manage with good or faulty judgment, with extensive or limited experience, or with exemplary or undesirable character. They come in all shapes, sizes, and temperaments. Some roar loudly at their

9

colleagues and subordinates; others speak softly. Still others send memos.

Inevitably there arises the question: Are managers born or made? In examining this question, researchers at General Motors, Sears Roebuck, Exxon, and other organizations have found that neither heredity nor environment is an absolute determinant, and that managerial effectiveness undoubtedly emerges from the interaction of the two. There is also abundant evidence that far more managers are made than are born. They are made through education, exposure, training, opportunities, guidance, appraisal, self-discipline, professionalism, and continuing growth and development on the job.

Some of those who are born could be stunted or even destroyed by a neurotic organization, top management cannibalism, reorganization orgies, and companies with hardening of the arteries. Some of those who are made could be unmade for the same reasons. When the organizational climate breeds distrust, cynicism, and insecurity, managers may retreat to one or another of the classified types listed above.

Parkinson's Law and the Peter Principle are often erroneously directed at the manager as a target. Parkinson's thesis is that work tends to expand to fill the time available for it, and that there is no real relationship between the number of officers available in an organization and the quantity of work done. This thesis is clearly more applicable to organizations than managers. Indeed, it is precisely bureaucratic civil service enterprises like the British Admiralty and the Foreign Office from which Parkinson draws his findings. Wasteful organizations breed wasteful managers. Similarly, the Peter Principle, which holds that each employee tends to rise to his level of incompetency, is more a criticism of the reward system than of individual managers. In organizations where there is drive, competitiveness, and growth, incompetency does *not* flourish. Again, most of Dr. Peter's findings are drawn from organizational structures such as universities, school systems, civil service agencies, and other organizations that are largely noncompetitive and that reward employees for longevity rather than competency.

We are concerned not so much with problem managers — those

who are maladjusted or emotionally ill — as with managers with problems. This distinction is essential. It is a common error to think in polar terms of competency and incompetency. More realistically, there are gradations of competency. Managers with problems are those who have difficulty in moving toward the different levels of competency required of them in their jobs. They are not emotional cripples. Their task is to overcome those barriers that limit their capabilities and hold them back. They need only to improve their outlook and enlarge their skills to measure up.

Techniques That Have Been Tried

Managers of business and industrial firms, managers of government bureaus, managers of nonprofit agencies and institutions, even managers of theological and religious organizations all have a common bond: the tough task of becoming a responsible and responsive manager, a real pro. Becoming a pro and responding as one in day-to-day management is not a solo effort.

There are three people who can help to shape the manager — his boss, himself, and a trusted subordinate. In this triad, the emphasis has long been on the man himself. Sink or swim; make or break; measure up or get out — the cult of self-made man persists. To be sure, in the long run the larger burden has to be on him. Only he can exercise the discipline needed to continue to grow as a manager. He cannot lean on a superior as a crutch. Nor can he ask a subordinate to serve as his full-time chaplain. Nevertheless, neither cumulative experience nor seniority in itself accomplishes this self-development, since a manager could be living through the wrong experiences or aping the wrong examples. Or he could just be spinning wheels, without realizing that he has struck a plateau point in his learning. Some men hold themselves down; others are held down by the organization. In either case, self-development is suppressed.

In one organization a sales supervisor who was turned down for a promotion argued that he had been a sales supervisor for five years. The director of personnel responded: "Your superiors believe otherwise. They contend that you have not been a supervisor for five years, but that you have been a supervisor one year, five times. You either stopped learning or haven't learned much at all since that first year."

In many companies emphasis is placed on another member of the triad—the manager's superior. He should be reviewing and observing the day-to-day activities of the subordinate manager; he should make a semiannual or annual appraisal of the man's performance and spotlight his strengths and weaknesses; and he should be coaching, counseling, and developing the subordinate so that he can grow as a manager. Indeed, the superior should exercise a good deal of caution in selecting the subordinate in the first place. Yet the selection process is often based on factors other than managerial potential—on seniority, technical ability, reliability, buddyism, nepotism, pressures from above, and so on.

Nevertheless, emphasis on the role of the superior is a sound doctrine. It is gospel that has been preached by the American Management Associations, the Harvard Business School, the U.S. Chamber of Commerce, and the National Association of Manufacturers. It is advocated by consultants in management education, trade associations that sponsor management seminars within their industries, and the many universities that conduct special programs to update managers. Despite the soundness of this view, results have been unimpressive. The management ranks are still riddled with deadwood, phonies, obsolescents, sadists, egotists, workaholics, and incompetents who should not be managing. Indeed, many should be charged with malpractice.

This leaves us with the third member of the triad—you. There are a number of things that you and other subordinates can do— meaningfully, productively, and with candor—to help the boss who is slipping. In doing so, you not only will be helping to save the man, your boss, but will be contributing to the welfare of the department and the economic well-being of the company.

THE CASE FOR THE SUBORDINATE HELPING HIS BOSS

If there were such a thing as the one best way of helping managers to rise above their mediocrity, you can be sure that some enterprising firm would long ago have declared: "Well, for heaven's sake, let's manufacture it and merchandise it." There is no one best way. Different managers fall into the trap of mediocrity in different ways for different reasons. Various routes have been taken to try to help the manager who is slipping. But few companies have tried the subordinate-to-boss route, the "you" route. Your aid, your needling, your support can help your boss perform better as a manager.

Too much has been expended on the amusing and simplistic theme of the "care and feeding" of managers. If there is any need for care and feeding, either it has been attended to long ago or it is now much too late. A much more productive approach is the "agricultural" view advocated by Saul Gellerman, adviser to a number of organizations on the problems of management motivation and development. He argues that managerial competence can be encouraged to grow in the same sense that a shrub or a tree can be encouraged to grow. Thus Gellerman is concerned not with the care and feeding of managers but with their growth and pruning. A manager's growth must be redirected where it is distorted or stunted, overextended to one side, or in the shadow of another object. Pruning is necessary to cut away blind spots, undesirable habits, and other impediments to sound development. The analogy is clear when you look at the manager as a growing professional who needs to mature and develop in his career.[1]

Just who is the "you" we are talking about? You are the key subordinate with immediate reporting relationship to the boss. You are the foreman, the specialist, the secretary, the deputy, or a supervisor. Or you may be the administrative assistant, a subordinate manager, a project leader, a staff specialist, or the assistant district manager. Whatever your position title, you are in a reporting relationship to the manager.

It makes little difference whether you are a newcomer or an oldtimer in the organization, male or female, college trained or up from the ranks, friendly or distant. The important thing is that you *want* to help your boss.

You don't have to like him in order to aid him in his maturation into a more professional manager. It helps, of course, if you do. But one does not have to like his boss to alert him to boobytraps, unwise commitments, or bad advice that could jeopardize the well-being of the department. You don't have to fraternize with him to impress upon him that by being dilatory in his actions he runs the risk of missing deadlines, incurring the ill will of other departments, and hurting the reputation of the work group. You don't have to like him to keep others off his back. You don't have

[1] Saul Gellerman, *Management by Motivation* (AMA, 1968), p. 107.

to be close to him to point out that by being a loner he runs the risk of doing a poor job of coordinating projects with other departments — projects whose success depends precisely on timely coordination.

Indeed, you will not like him when he is greedy. But when his greediness breeds low morale, you may have to offer the cue that not giving credit to subordinates for their good work could lead to demoralization in the department and even the loss of good men. Or when he plays the game of secrecy, you may have to let him know that there simply must be more communication in order to get jobs done well and on time.

Why You?

There are several cogent reasons why you should be a party to your boss's growth and development. First, his superiors expect more of him than just his output in terms of production, sales, or paperwork — important as this is. They also want his responsiveness, his ideas, his rapport, his energies, his special knowledge, and his pursuit of goals and objectives. As they expect this of him, so by implication they expect it of every member of his department. You are part of that constituency.

Second, to the extent that you enable your boss to measure up to these expectations, you enable yourself and the department to look good. Both employees and managers share in the real rewards that result from higher departmental achievement.

Third, and the credo of this book, it is the job of every subordinate to make his boss look good in the eyes of *his* boss. Contrary to the personnel department's counsel, you should be more interested in your boss's job description than in your own. That is, you should be more sensitive to who is breathing down his neck, the condition of his in-basket, the mounting number of priorities he faces, when he is meeting deadlines on time and when he is late, and other aspects of his managerial task.

The job of the manager is to be effective; this is what he is paid for. Managerial effectiveness can be learned and, as Peter Drucker contends, it *must* be learned. You, the subordinate, can assist in the learning process. After all, as his subordinate you are very much within his orbit. You bear the impact of his plans (good or bad), his approaches to problem solving (moving toward or retreating from), his work assignments (challenging or routine), and his changes (well or poorly executed). You bear the brunt of his outbursts, frustrations, and failures. And you share in his successes and triumphs.

What Can You Help Him With?

We would do well to begin with the ways you *can't* help your boss. You can't change your boss's body chemistry, temperament, instincts, ego, the early lessons he learned at his grandfather's feet, or other deep-seated influences. Don't even attempt it. The only ways to change these are through psychotherapy, chemotherapy, religious conversion, or brain surgery. You are not equipped to do it. In short, you cannot remake him.

What you can do is to help him become a more responsible and responsive manager. As a member of his team, you can help him redirect his energies and time, his goals and priorities, his risk taking, his judgments, and his delegations. You can influence his ability to adjust to change, his relationships with other departments, his use of authority, his evaluation and control, and his overall contribution to the company. In time you may enable him to reassess his responsibilities as a manager and perhaps even to formulate a sound philosophy of how to run his department. These gains will in turn enable him to cut down on or to cope better with some of the more frustrating aspects of his job. They may make him aware of some of his blind spots as a manager. With this kind of self-awareness, he may even be able to manage his emotions.

In short, in helping your boss through positive and constructive redirection of his time and energy, you enable him to help himself — to develop a different outlook on his job and to improve his ability to deal with change, modernization, and growth in the company. Who knows — you may even be accountable in part for his promotion to another position! It has happened before.

All managers are in transition, and all have their share of difficulties. For most managers, and probably for your own boss, it is not so much a case of incompetency as one of limited competency, inflexibility, and erratic behavior—things that can be changed. Your boss may not have the potential for moving up into the executive ranks, but your department does have potential. By helping your boss, you will be helping your department to grow, produce results, and acquit itself well with top management.

Essentials in Your Relationship with the Boss

As stated earlier, you don't have to like your boss to work with him. It helps, of course, if you do. But far more important is the quality of your relationship with him, and this has to be built both ways. The key word is mutuality. These are the essential ingredients in establishing a sound relationship with your boss:

Mutual knowledge: of what's going on, what's due to come up.
Mutual responsibility: for goals, assignments, performance.
Mutual concern: for worthwhile and productive results.
Mutual confidence and respect: in and for one another.
Mutual contribution: to the economic good of the company.

This kind of relationship is not built easily, nor does it come by wishing it. It has to be cultivated slowly and genuinely.

For all your efforts to build a sound relationship with your boss and to make him look good, in the long run he will have to take final action—to make the decision, present the program, or recommend the solution. Therefore, let him project his own image in his work and in his relationships with others. Let him impose his *own* image as he moves into final action on any of these. You have done all you can to help him achieve a better image and be more confident and persuasive. From that point on let him be his own man.

Even if you do succeed in establishing a good relationship with him, all will not be sweetness and light. There will be occasions of disagreement or misunderstanding. You and he have to learn the art of disagreeing agreeably. Disagree, if you have to, about goals, strategies, tactics, approaches, and methods, and in this way keep personalities relegated to the background. And when you disagree, do it tactfully. Learn the facts, do your homework, and be sure of your ground so that you can reinforce the substance of your viewpoint. Finally, learn to be flexible and teach him to bend a bit now and then. Rigidity is a nasty barrier. It precludes mutuality.

What's in It for You, the Subordinate?

We have already established the rationale for why a subordinate should try to help his boss. But the question remains: Why should a subordinate do it when he is not being paid for it? In fact, there is much compensation—nonfinancial compensation—to be gained. In helping your boss and making him look good to his boss, you should realize nonfinancial or psychological rewards such as these:

Gaining an opportunity to practice your craft or profession better and with more satisfaction.

Having greater peace of mind (rather than frustration) on the job.

Having the satisfaction of being listened to and seeing some of your ideas put into practice.

Acquiring more and increasingly diversified experience in the work setting.

Gaining self-esteem, respect, and ego fulfillment from participating, consulting, and conferring in the decision-making process.

Developing less strained working relationships.

Promoting better interdepartmental relationships and thereby enhancing the reputation of your department.

Seeing some of the department's more important priorities achieved.

Gaining pride and security from knowing that your department
is doing well and is achieving recognition.

To be sure, some of these rewards could lead to direct or indirect
financial rewards as well.

Finally, in helping your boss you will be helping yourself—to
break out of the parochialism of your specialty; to learn more
about planning, decision making, and control; and to handle
projects of increasing difficulty and magnitude. You too will gain
in experience and maturity. As opportunities arise for advancement, promotion, and transfer, or as promising openings appear
in other companies in the industry, you will have slowly but surely
readied yourself to be in the running.

These, then, are the rewards. This is the only candid answer to
the question of what's in it for a subordinate.

Any Limits?

Are there limits to what you should do to help your boss? Yes.
First, in your commitment to make him look good in his professional life, don't step into his social life. Remember that in serving as a catalyst, in getting him to change his outlook toward his
responsibilities and his performance, you will at times appear to
him to be an irritant and an upstart. Don't compound it by in-
truding on his social life. Don't interfere with his shenanigans in
the office, the plant, the department. Specifically, don't get involved in his indiscretions in dating women in the office or carrying on an extramarital affair.

Stay out of it. He won't take good advice, and he will resent bad
advice. He will misinterpret your interest as interference in his life,
and you will undermine your relationship with him. Don't tell his
wife; don't indulge in the gossip in the car pool; don't try to be his
chaplain; don't defend him and don't attack him. Just be neutral.
Stand on the sidelines and watch the drama unfold. Even if you
could help in one particular instance by showing him how his
indiscretion with a secretary is hurting the reputation of the department, this Don Juan will get involved with another woman the

next time round. Just let him draw his own noose around his career and his personal life.

Other limits have to do with his health, his family, his debts, his politics, and other areas of his personal life. If he unloads his problems on you now and then, give him the therapeutic satisfaction of listening. Just listen — no more than that. The case for your making your boss look good is sound only to the extent that it is concerned with his competency as a manager.

THE SPECTRUM OF BOSSES

The spectrum of bosses in the organized (and the unorganized or disorganized) enterprise is broad enough to encompass all kinds of people. There are the inexperienced, the insecure, the indifferent, and the unsuccessful. There are the seasoned, the confident, the enthusiastic, and the high achievers. Bosses come in all shapes, sizes, and temperaments. They come from different occupational backgrounds—from sales, manufacturing, traffic, finance, research and development, office management, and other areas. They come from different cultural backgrounds— American, European, Latin American, and so forth. Because of their origin, background, and experience, they behave in different ways and take on different managerial styles or patterns.

Within this spectrum of bosses, there are many whom you need not, cannot, or should not help. Clearly, you need not help the boss who is of proven competency, professionalism, and promotability. He has made it without your guidance and will probably continue to do so. You should try to influence him now and then on specific points in your relationship. There is always room for improvement and there are always new challenges that must be met. But for the most part you need play only an occasional role in helping this boss. At the other pole, you cannot and should not attempt to help those bosses who are unhelpable. Among these are the "problem managers"—the neurotics, the tyrants, the defeatists. Others include the nepotists, whose position in the company is assured because of family relationships; the untouchables, who have more power than managers should have in an organization; and the coasters, who are pasturing out the next few years until their retirement.

In his case studies of over 300 managers, Harry Levinson classifies as among those bosses who cannot be helped managers who are mentally ill and managers who display hostility as a conspicuous symptom. In addition, Levinson categorizes as maladaptive those managers who have limited personalities—the anxious ones, the rigid ones, the dependent ones, and the impulsive ones—and those who are misplaced—who either have been placed in the wrong position (the hapless ones) or have been outdistanced by their jobs (the helpless ones).[1] There are many others, quite acceptable managers with specific characteristics which you cannot do much about. They are too many to identify, and their whims and idiosyncrasies are too varied to catalog.

It is important, then, to limit your efforts to those bosses who *can* be helped. With this limitation in mind, let's examine some recognizable profiles.

[1] Harry Levinson, "Who Is to Blame for Maladaptive Managers?" *Harvard Business Review* (November–December 1965), pp. 143–153.

Profiles:
THESE BOSSES CAN BE HELPED

The "Nice Guy, But..." Manager

The Contentment Syndrome

Background Profile

The nice-guy manager needs to be helped for several reasons: First, he tends to mistake soft management for humanistic management. Second, he often does not look good to his peers and his own boss. As a result, his image and his position on the management team suffer. Finally, in his gentleness and agreeableness, he leaves the department deficient in leadership. All these things have an impact on you and others in the department.

It should be noted at the outset that there is something to be said in behalf of the nice-guy manager. It is sometimes a welcome relief to work with a boss who generates friendliness, treats employees with respect and dignity, and even sets an example of ethical behavior. The nice-guy boss does not want to offend anyone. He displays genuine interest in and concern for his people, listens to their woes, extends his good wishes to those who are leaving the company, and is always ready to fraternize with a beer or a whiskey sour. He exudes agreeableness and even makes it contagious. The adherents of Blake and Mouton would label him as 1,1—the sociable, country-club type. Those affiliated with the sensitivity school in management would probably tag him as a laissez-faire manager.

Tendencies

For all his agreeableness and spreading of cheer, the nice-guy manager has certain tendencies that can hurt the department and you, his subordinate. In his desire not to be pushy or aggressive, he fails to assert himself sufficiently on important issues— issues on which he *should* take a stand. In the simplistic belief that anything communicated is intended for the general welfare, he is unwilling to question or doubt directives from higher up. Quite comfortable in expressing pleasant feelings, he avoids criticizing or disagreeing with others. In the naive belief that all managers are expected to cooperate with one another, he finds rivalries painful. He leans toward actions that are likely to be popular and easily accepted rather than toward more rigorous actions that are subject to debate. Bad news can demolish him. He seeks to avoid grievances at all costs. He is encumbered with deadwood employees, but his gentle, easy-going nature prevents him from terminating them.

Very often the nice-guy manager becomes a patsy. Bosses and colleagues in the management ranks get him overcommitted to work, schedules, committees, and special projects. They also try to unload their incompetent or insubordinate employees on his department, using it as a dumping ground. Like the girl in that classic song in *Oklahoma,* he's just a guy who can't say no. He is easy prey to these seductions.

The nice-guy boss tends to cover up his deficiencies with trappings such as these:

"It's too late in life to fight."
"The company has been good to us; let's be good to it."
"I know they mean well."
"Let's divide the pressure—too much on one man is not good."
"There's enough gloom around; let's try to get some enjoyment out of what we're doing."
"What else is there in life but friendship?"
"It's a bad deal, but we can live with it."
"I've seen top management teams come and go, but I'm still here."

Living by platitudes, turning the other cheek, playing the role of the in-company Billy Graham, and being overly indulgent about human frailties—this is the way of the nice-guy manager, but it is also an escape from reality.

All these tendencies can and often do backfire. Who pays the price for it? You. Your associates. The department. You pay for it in disappointments, reversals, stagnation. You come out on the short end of negotiations; you find yourself deluged by paperwork. There is little chance that you will grow in your craft or profession under such a manager. This is the essence of the "nice guy, but . . ." pattern.

Analysis

How does a manager come to be a nice guy? It could be just his natural temperament and inclination. This is simply the way he is, being himself. Or it could be that he is undergoing a period of emotional or physical stress. Another explanation is that someone has conned him into the belief that being a nice guy is a mark of managerial leadership. Or he may have realized that he has reached his ceiling, that he is going no further in the company. If this is to be his lot, he finds some satisfaction in being resignedly pleasant and making it pleasant for others in the department. Some clinicians have suggested more subtle psychological explanations of his behavior. The nice-guy boss has a desire to project himself as a father figure, to play the paternalistic role. The workplace is his haven, his refuge from the harshness of life at home with an irascible wife or errant children. Or he is simply a man who needs to be loved.

Whatever the reasons, they are not that important. What *is* important is the "but" in the "nice guy, but . . ." pattern. Inherent in the "but" are the limitations, the boobytraps that beset the nice-guy manager and the vulnerable position in which he places the department. In the competitive organizational climate, life will inevitably become difficult for such a manager and the naiveté of his "Gee, whiz" management.

The nice-guy boss has a distorted concept of human relations in management. Gentleness and contentment are not the goals of an economic enterprise. Nor are they the obligations of those charged with managerial responsibility to direct the enterprise, although at times they are effective as a means of achieving organizational goals. Nice-guy leadership does not necessarily raise the morale and productivity of those in the department. As evidenced in the studies of the University of Michigan's Institute for Social Research, there may or may not be a correlation between sociability, morale, and productivity. It all depends on what subordinates want. Employees may be contented with an easy, agreeable, pressureless environment with little in the way of standards of production. In this case the nice-guy manager will generate good morale — but probably little productivity. On the other hand, subordinates may seek satisfaction that comes from taking pride in their work, from performing effectively with co-workers, and from doing interesting and challenging tasks. They may wish to use their talents and skills, to grow on the job, and to gain the recognition and reward that comes with proven performance. Here nice-guy leadership will lead to neither better morale nor higher productivity.

Sound human relations in management is concerned with tapping motivationally the best in subordinates' capabilities, attitudes, and experience and applying those skills toward achieving corporate goals. It is also concerned with effective communication, group cohesion and productivity, and resourceful and positive ways of reconciling differences and misunderstandings.

The nice-guy boss also has a misdirected concept of getting along with others. He fails to accept the fact that conflict as well as cooperation is part of the reality of managerial life, and that conflicts must be faced and resolved. In extreme cases, he may even default in managerial authority, fail to exercise controls, or make only decisions that please people and are readily acceptable.

How to Work With and Help This Boss

First, some key don'ts for you, the subordinate, in working with the nice-guy boss:

☐ Don't ape him. You will only add to the general softness and deterioriation of the department.

☐ Don't be entirely contented with the easy-going atmosphere, much as you may like it. It's illusory. You will pay a high price for it in the long run. Your skills and abilities will go stale, and you will not develop and grow on the job. Look out for your own future.

☐ Don't take advantage of the nice guy and his flair for fraternization and agreeableness. Be a party to it, if you enjoy the camaraderie, but keep it within bounds of reasonableness.

Here are several guidelines for what you can do positively for the nice-guy boss and how you can make him look good to his boss:

☐ Get across to him, slowly but surely, the lesson spelled out in the background profile: that there is a difference between sound motivational management and soft-hearted, paternalistic management. Make him aware of his distortion of the human relations concept and alert him to the boobytraps.

☐ Impress upon him that respect is more important than popularity. He could, possibly, have both, but it is far more important that he have respect. Make him aware of the kind of respect that comes with being on top of the job and its responsibilities — with being able to plan and control well, to spot pending trouble and deal with it effectively, and to tap the best in his people and harness their talents, special skills, energies, and cooperation toward achieving departmental goals. Tell him that in equating good relationships with good management he is only partially correct. Good management is more closely linked with good results. And results may occur because of or in spite of good relationships.

☐ If you find he is prone to make commitments that result in excessive workloads or other difficulties for those in the department, get on his back about making promises. He shouldn't have much trouble understanding the simple caution that he should avoid making promises he cannot keep.

☐ Now and then shatter the country-club atmosphere. At the weekly staff meeting spark some honest debate, give-and-take criticism, or even a shouting match. Hopefully, you and others will come out of the meeting shaking hands and nodding mutual respect. During the meeting, needle co-workers for evidence, substantiation, and justification of their views just to shake up the easy-going climate that the nice-guy manager engenders. As he chairs the meeting, he will get the message that dissent, criticism, challenge, and provocation can produce good results without endangering man-to-man relationships. Let him see that there is value in creative discontent.

☐ Relieve him of the pain that comes with making difficult decisions. Friendships can ruin business when personal ties prevent a manager from facing up to a decision. A manager can give consideration to personal ties or friendships with his men, of course, but in the final analysis a good decision has to be based on objectivity rather than sentiment. So don't let his friendship with you (or with others in the department) impair his ability to make decisions objectively and soundly.

□ Encourage him to make decisions (on schedules, facilities, assignments, budgets, controls, and so on) that will be of value to the entire department rather than tilted in favor of you or any other individual.

□ Help him go to bat for you. As part of his pattern of good fellow-ship, the nice-guy manager will want to make a pitch on your behalf to higher-ups. The question is not *whether* he goes to bat, but *how* he goes to bat for you. In his aversion to debate and his fear of offending others, he may go about it very super-ficially and not present your case as well as he should. He could be quite honest in bringing the matter before his su-periors, but he will be dishonest if he makes only a token pre-sentation. If necessary, fortify him with facts and rebuttals, do some of his homework for him, and make sure he is armed fully. After he has met with his superiors, get as straightforward an account as possible of what happened. If he comes out of the meeting with a favorable result, good. If the result is unfavor-able, probe him to find out what happened and how it was handled; then find an appropriate time for him to take another crack at it. You are entitled to this kind of communication.

□ Serve as antennae for him. Make him aware of those who are trying to pull a fast one on him, to dump some disagreeable work on his department, or to institute some "minor" organiza-tional shift that will leave him holding the bag. In his innocent and trusting nature, this man needs your help. Raise the red flag when you suspect that some mischief is going on.

□ Stress that doing battle is part of organizational life and that there is no point in wishing it away. While man-to-man rela-tionships may be quite friendly, the road to sound interdepart-mental or headquarters-field relationships is not an easy one. There will be times when the nice-guy boss will have to do battle because of competing demands, limited resources, and other problems. Bolster his courage to enter a battle when there is need for it, and help him develop the best strategy and tactics. All he needs is to witness the infighting firsthand and come out a winner once or twice, and he no longer will need any bolstering. Persuade him that he is doing battle about *issues* and not so much with people. This approach may allay some of his fears about offending others.

☐ Get him to think more realistically in terms of negotiating rather than compromising. The nice-guy manager fancies himself as being good at compromising. Compromise, to him, has a ring of agreeableness. Get him to dispel this notion. He may not enjoy twisting the other fellow's arm during negotiations, but neither should he allow his own arm to be twisted.

☐ When he goes into a prospective compromise session with another department or unit, caution him on what you feel cannot or should not be compromised in the best interests of the department. Discuss with him what the department can yield on without too much loss and what it hopes to gain from the negotiations. Emphasize that not everything can be ironed out at one sitting and that sometimes it is best to call an impasse and try again later. Negotiations may leave him bruised, weary, and confused. Under such circumstances, he may not think straight or exercise good judgment. Urge him to pull out and schedule another session when he can think more clearly and make better judgments. You must protect your boss, the nice guy, in such situations. The stakes are high, not only for him but for you and the department as a whole.

☐ Do what you can, with the cooperation of others, to spot a complaint early, before it emerges into a full-blown grievance. The nice-guy manager views a grievance as a personal blow to his ego. How could it possibly happen in his department? Yet grievances do arise in the strains and tensions of the work environment. There is abundant evidence that up to 80 percent of all incipient grievances can be amicably settled at the first-line level of supervision. It is the responsibility of you and other subordinates to help out in this kind of preventive management. When there is a formal system for resolving grievances by carrying them to the second, third, and fourth levels—which then involve your boss's superiors, the personnel department, and others—his ego will be threatened even more severely. Spare him this exposure and grief. Try to deal with complaints at the first stage.

☐ Reinforce the view that good planning and good controls are essential for departmental performance, and that they are subject to revision. Controls are not inviolate. In his aversion for tightening up on people, the nice-guy boss will be reluctant to install new controls. If the controls are timely, necessary, and well designed, back up their installation and urge him to give them a fair test. Impress upon him that controls imposed from above are not necessarily a mark of distrust, and that in implementing such controls he is not being distrustful of his people. Any sound control is intended as a managerial tool to improve operations through obtaining earlier and more objective feedback of results.

☐ Prod him to get away for a one-day or two-day seminar on human relations in management. It will be good for his continuing education as a manager to learn, with other business managers and through a source outside the company, more motivational factors (employees' desires for challenge, opportunity, responsibility, pride in achievement, utilization of abilities, recognition, and so on) other than those he assumed were motivation enough in the nice-guy climate.

Some of these guidelines will not be easy to pursue. Even the gentle and agreeable nice-guy manager will at times show resistance for one of two reasons. First, he may be quite inexperienced as a manager and hence may believe that being a nice guy is the only way to win friends and influence people. Second, he may find tough-minded management difficult. The term "tough-minded" here refers not to threatening, harsh, or domineering behavior, but to tough-mindedness in terms of setting high standards and goals and expecting results. Let's hope the nice-guy manager is not too fragile to take the latter course.

If his resistance persists, you may have to let him go it alone for a while. But if he rides his boat into perilous waters, be a friend and bail him out. Hopefully, he will have learned something from the experience.

Finally, the nice guy seldom has the worry that a subordinate is out to get his job. He may be quite right on this score. However, if he continues to be intent on nice-guy management rather than results management, it will not be a subordinate but someone in top management who will knock the props from under him. Soon he will be replaced by another man with a different managerial style. So do what you can to work effectively with this boss and help him salvage his job.

The Panic-Button Boss

Fasten Your Seat Belts;
We Expect Some Turbulence

Background Profile

Those who work for the panic-button manager might as well come to work each day not only with their brown-bag lunches but also with an explosometer. They could use it to get a reading on just when the boss is about to explode—and run for cover.

This boss is a familiar management specimen. His daily behavior is characterized by a driving pace, snap judgments, frantic telephone calls, and constant crises. He might as well join the Fourteenth Hook and Ladder Brigade, for he is always putting out fires. Fire fighting is his forte. While putting out the fires, he may look heroic to his people. Little do they know that he is an arsonist—that he starts these fires. Lack of planning and disdain for real priorities are the matches that kindle the flames. Everything is big, and everything is urgent. Management by crisis is his specialty. Breakdowns, complaints, absenteeism, long-distance calls, expected VIP visits, missing records, the slow pace of new workers—all are viewed as critical emergencies, and he moves swiftly to press the panic button. Nor is the button pressed softly. It is often accompanied by some showmanship—tantrums, profanity, muttered threats.

He lives the fantasy of the "take charge" manager. This is part of the egotism fostered in the fantasy. He generally makes seat-of-the-pants, intuitive decisions. Everything is a hot priority, so let's get on top of it—fast. We'll take a gamble. He does his own bellhopping, taking on the most immediate item he sees.

Nothing escapes his attention, no matter how small or trivial. He runs a one-man show. To a very real extent he is out to prove the wisdom of Murphy's Law in management: if anything can possibly go wrong in this place, it will. He is ever alert to what might go wrong and ever ready to get on top of it quickly. In running his one-man show, he breeds distrust among subordinates. His is a detailed, one-track mind.

Our hero builds his own pressures and denies himself the time for simple essentials. His lunch often consists of a sandwich and coffee at the desk or a quick snack at Gerry's In-and-Out Luncheonette down the street. The subject of vacations is taboo with him. If and when he does go on vacation, this self-styled indispensable gives his wife fits after only three days. He'll sneak out of the beach cottage with his trouser pocket full of quarters and dimes and run to the nearest public telephone booth to call the office. He has to assure himself that things are not going too badly in the department and that he can stretch the vacation by another day or two. In the office Rolaids and Bufferin are his reinforcements. His secretary is equipped with this do-it-yourself medical kit, which she keeps in her drawer.

Things get done in his department, to be sure. But there is little or no planning in the buzz-saw atmosphere he creates. Nor can he see the forest, for he is constantly working at a tree here and there. Employees work under considerable tension, wondering who will be the victim of the next outburst, and they regard a successful day as one in which the clock strikes 5 P.M. with fewer crises than the day before.

Life can be absurd at times, and working for the panic-button boss is one of life's more sparkling absurdities. Moreover, putting in more years than one should under this boss could become a very grim experience. Yet one finds the panic-button boss in all types of companies—indeed, he is a living legend in many industries.

Tendencies

The impact of the panic-button boss on you, other subordinates, and the department as a whole is quite vivid. In running his one-man show he violates two important principles of management: he doesn't keep others informed when they need to be informed, and he ignores the abilities and talents of those in the department. These two violations are enough to bring an indictment. In the course of generating a panic-button atmosphere and putting pressure on himself, he induces fatigue, pressure, and unnecessary stress on others. This is not appreciated, and many a muted "s.o.b." is muttered during the day, you can be sure.

The scurrying around and the last-minute solutions inevitably lead to a number of mistakes. The panic-button boss will try either to cover up his mistakes and redouble his efforts or to pin the blame on others. There is no time for thoughtful, considered judgments. Don't act; just react—with seat-of-the-pants judgments and expedient solutions. Everyone pays a price for the erratic decisions. The unwillingness or the inability to plan well is reflected in unrealistic targets in sales, services, production schedules, budgets, and other matters. Whether undertargeted or overtargeted, unrealistic goals lead to unhappy outcomes. Moreover, his lack of planning and control creates many breakdowns in the department. Often a troubleshooting team is dispatched to locate the breakdown and take temporary measures to correct it. Fix it rather than cure it is the order of the day. Under the pressure of crises, real or fancied, this boss finds little time for thinking and reflecting on what and how the department is doing. As an idea or suggestion is put forth, he is generally quick to interrupt and either dismiss it as unworkable or hold it for some other time. One senses the stifling of ideas under this one-man rule, just as one senses the mistrust and the underutilization of the abilities and skills of people.

The department he directs is often characterized more by disorganization than organization. It shows up as an organization on paper, of course, but he will tamper with the structure at will as he reacts to stresses and doubts. Responsibilities and authority of subordinates are kept fuzzy, yet he demands accountability for results. In the disorganization he often assigns work to the handiest guy around rather than to the one most able or technically qualified. Organization isn't all that important, he concludes. All one needs is good people—and good people are those who nurse his ego.

In summation, this boss breathes to those around him, day in and day out, a sense of shared common disaster in the department, but without letting on that he is a party to most of the disasters. That secret is as open as the Atlantic.

Analysis

This kind of profile makes the panic-button boss a vulnerable target at which to throw darts. However, it does not necessarily imply that he is evil or incompetent. Yet one is tempted to do some analysis of this fellow and to see what makes him tick. The psychological roots of his behavior could be many. Some clinicians suggest that his tantrums and outbursts are a retreat to infantilism and the need for a mother to cater to his needs. Others pose the speculation that all his busyness and excitement are a way of compensating for an otherwise dull life away from the job. More serious researchers identify the panic-button boss as one who is running a mad race with himself, driven to it and uncertain as to why. Other researchers see his behavior as an attempt to emulate a relentless, authoritarian father. Those who work in his department see him as a little man trying to look big. His own bosses accept him as a driver. And if you were to ask him to explain his behavior, he would be likely to say quite simply: "This is the only way to do it, to get ahead."

Perhaps we can gain some clue to his behavior in this comment by a ship's captain during an ocean voyage. "Ladies and gentlemen," the captain told his passengers, "I have two announcements, one bad and the other good. The bad news is that we're off course and probably lost; the good news is that we're making very good time." This could well be the dilemma of the panic-button manager.

A closer look at this profile reveals that there is more than one type of manager who is prone to panic-button leadership. There is, first, the undisciplinarian. He is unable to discipline himself or to govern his time, energies, emotions, or work habits. Consequently each new day at the office or the plant is a repeat of another unplanned day, filled with erratic and frantic efforts to cope with problems. He does not so much manage work as handle a chain reaction of incidents from 9 A.M. to 5 P.M. It is a good guess that he relishes each incident as an opportunity to gratify his need to look like the take-charge manager, a self-styled hero.

Another type of boss prone to panic-button management is the nondelegator, the do-it-all-yourself man. In the illusion that nothing less than his personal involvement in every activity is essential, he parcels out to subordinates only routine duties. His ego won't let him accept the fact that there are others in the department who can take on more than just routine tasks—who can indeed handle a good portion of what reaches his desk. The problem is that he won't let go. His reasons for refusing to allocate departmental matters to subordinates are many and varied: he might lose control; subordinates might make an error; it takes time to explain the project or assignment; subordinates are not ready to take on such delegations and are much too busy with their own regular workloads; he could do it faster and better himself. Behind such rationalizations and alibis is perhaps the fear that he may have to credit a subordinate with a job well done. This sharing of credit or accomplishment runs counter to his ego, his need to gain all the plaudits and recognition as the one indispensable man.

In any event, the nondelegator often finds himself a drowning man. He is pulled down by the weight of all these responsibilities — the priorities, deadlines, projects, commitments, visits, and reports — and struggles under the delusion that he, and only he, can do it all. The result: a burdensome workload on one man, a frenzied effort to get to things on a catch-as-catch-can basis, an erratic approach to handling items in his in-basket, a last-ditch effort to be prepared for a staff meeting, and a general atmosphere of panic in the department.

A third kind of boss prone to panic-button management is the proprietor. This type of boss regards the business as his own proprietorship, whether it is or not. He recites this theme to employees ad nauseam and doesn't permit them to forget it: "I built the business (or plant, unit, department) the hard way. It took blood, sweat, and tears, but I did it. And now that I've brought it to where it is, I'll call the shots and run it my own way." He fails to mention that in addition to the holy three of blood, sweat, and tears, it took some bank loans, piracy, stepping over bruised bodies or demolished careers, bailing out by friends, union payoffs, and close brushes with the law.

If he is the proprietor of his own business, his mission in life is not to manage more professionally but to pass on the business to Freddy, his eldest son. Freddy is now a Zen Buddhist and has settled into the family den with his co-religionists to engage in daily meditation with the inner self. Or, to hear Freddy's side of the story: "What the hell is it that I want out of life, anyway? I'm only certain of one thing—I don't want to inherit and have to run my father's business.''

How to Work With and Help This Boss

First, several don'ts for you, the subordinate, in working with the panic-button boss:

☐ Don't give him fuel for more fires. Try to improve your own performance and to make judgments that are accurate and as foolproof as possible—so that not even smoke, let alone fire, emerges.

☐ Don't get trapped into highly emotional arguments with him. In an atmosphere already charged with tension, blame-fixing will be this boss's common reaction. You may be innocent of the charge. Defend yourself. However, if you find that he is gunning for an argument, don't get drawn in. You will only add more heat to the fire. You can't get your point across to an angry man, and anger begets more anger. So hold your cool and carry on your defense later in the day.

☐ Don't sneer at a one-man show. Some one-man shows are very good and have favorable organizational and economic results. Granted that they are few in number and exceptional. Nevertheless, snide remarks and mockery by subordinates will not change the style of the panic-button boss. If you are going to rebel against the one-man show because of its ill effects, do so productively—not by off-the-cuff remarks.

If you see little hope for change, don't stay on. Bear in mind that when organizational crises are caused by *one* panic-button boss, your boss, there is some possibility for change. If, however, the company is infested with a corps of panic-button bosses, get out. You, and several hundred employees like you, are not likely to change a thing. Pursue your career elsewhere and scan the press regularly for news of your former company's demise.

THE PANIC-BUTTON BOSS

Here are several guidelines to what you can do positively to make this boss look good to his boss:

☐ Lighten his load; give him some relief. Intercept as many items of business as you reasonably can at your level (even if you have only marginal or doubtful authority to do so) and take care of them with dispatch. If they are not vital, don't even let them get to the fire fighter's attention. The safeguard, of course, is to handle them competently. If you do, he won't even bother, in his disorganized organization, to ask whether or not you overstepped your authority.

☐ Anticipate things that might backfire or cause trouble. Handle them well in advance so that you can forestall a possible crisis. No organization is immune to crises, and in some cases crises are necessary. But for your boss's sake and for the sake of the company, avoid unnecessary problems.

☐ Be cautious about making promises or commitments that you can't keep — whether to vendors, customers, shippers, inspectors, contractors, visitors, or your own employees. If you have any doubt, clear it first with your boss. This in itself may reduce the panic-button pushing.

☐ Improve the controls at your own desk or unit. Make sure that your operations are sufficiently orderly and efficient so that information, records, correspondence, data, contracts, or other source materials can be reached promptly. And be sure they are up to date and accurate. It's bad enough that your boss's operations are disorderly and chaotic; don't compound the problem. In short, improve your own work habits.

☐ Run interference for your boss. If your antennae detect trouble coming (a potentially unhappy customer, possible faulty computer input, a threatened work stoppage), get together with your colleagues and see what can be done. You may be able to solve the problem before it gets to the fire fighter.

☐ Respect time. Most activities in business have a deadline, a schedule, a sequence — some time designation by hour, day, week, or month. Develop an effective tickler system or red-flag system to serve as an alarm as to what's due when. Too many panic-button incidents arise from the simple "Oh, it slipped my mind." Don't rely exclusively on the system, on your memory, or on a secretary. All three may be needed. Use them regularly and don't let deadlines get out of hand.

☐ Let the tail wag the dog. Do your own planning well and keep your priorities in clear view at all times. Install timely and effective controls of your operations, know when trouble is headed your way, coordinate and confer with others as needed, and perform competently at your level. Get your associates or other supervisors to do the same over a period of time—all through the appeal that there must be a way to beat panic-button management. After a while, you will all be working with less pressure and with fewer crises than before—not because of your boss's leadership but in spite of it. And he may eventually get the message that you and others do not accept panic-button management as part of the daily routine. As a special measure for emergencies, yes; as a way of life, no.

☐ Get his ear. Wherever and whenever you can—whether on the job or off, in his office or in the corridor, before the workday begins or after it is over—if the occasion warrants, get him to listen. The egotist does not listen readily. Yet if you are to rescue him from his mistake, you must get his ear.

If he persists in warding off one-to-one conversations under the guise that something has just broken loose and he must get to the scene of action immediately, then try the mobilization approach. Get together with several concerned co-workers and descend on him as a group to discuss an anticipated problem before another crisis erupts. Don't be deterred by his secretary and don't tell her what it's all about. Her instinct will be to protect him. So break through, discreetly or boldly, to get to the boss. You will be protecting him in a far more genuine and meaningful way than she can. At first he may worry that this is a group grievance, a collective announcement of a showdown. Beset by real or imagined crises, he doesn't want to be burdened with additional headaches. It will come to him as a relief to find that this is not a grievance or a showdown after all, and that you and others have joined forces to help him out of a potential trouble spot. The prospects are good that he will listen.

After the first time, the mobilized approach won't have the

same dramatic effect, but keep using it as necessary. The chances are good that he will listen more than he did in the past. Indeed, the approach may become an accepted channel of communication in the department. It certainly beats regular staff meetings — but then, the panic-button boss doesn't believe in staff meetings.

Special Focus

In addition to these guidelines, it will be necessary to get across to the panic-button boss some new approaches in managing the department and managing himself. It won't be easy, but it has to be done. These new approaches, though intended for him, must be directed through you if you are to have any hope of counteracting his panic-button management.

Focus on preventive management. Stress the importance of getting beneath the surface of the incident, the mishap, the breakdown that caused the finger to press the panic button. Getting beneath the surface means analyzing what has happened, discovering the real causes, and testing out alternative procedures so that the department can take corrective measures now and preventive measures in the future.

After a football game, the coach and his players hold a "skull session" to determine just what happened. The game is projected on a screen in slow motion so that the players can analyze who missed his cue, who should have covered whom, and what plays failed. This technique can also be valuable in management. Get across to your boss the importance of holding a skull session after a troublesome incident. During the session, do not devalue what happened; rather, stress the lessons the department has learned from the incident and move on to corrective and preventive measures. Both you and your boss will be astonished at the reduction in the number of crises. If necessary, urge him to develop an operating manual outlining the new and better techniques for averting trouble so that every newcomer in the department will know how to proceed.

Preventive management involves taking a look at the department's scheduling, staffing, work assignments, production standards, and procedures and reexamining them periodically to make any changes needed. It also involves better planning, coordination, and control.

In short, have your boss take heed of philosopher George Santayana's counsel: Those who do not learn from the mistakes of the past are doomed to repeat them.

Focus on plans and priorities. Your boss is paid mainly for making decisions. Decisions on plans and priorities are equal in importance only to decisions regarding people. Impress upon him that plans and priorities are the roadmap for your department; without them, you and others cannot move forward. Directly or deviously, get him to set out his plans on paper and to develop a balanced program of long, intermediate, and short-term plans. For the present, urge him to focus on clearly stated short-term plans (for the next six months or so) and intermediate-term plans (for a year or two). Later he may be needled by top management to come up with long-term objectives and plans. There is a correlation between aimlessness and panic situations, so keep coaxing him into developing plans.

Focus on the role of the boss. If he is uncertain about his role as a boss and if top management has failed to clarify that role for him, help him to do so. There is a difference between doing and managing, between being energetic and being effective, between wasting time on the wrong jobs and working on the right jobs, and between acting like a mechanic, clerk, or technician and acting like a manager. Get him to see the difference.

He should be engaged more in directing others than in doing things himself, more in planning than in troubleshooting, more in assessing than in threatening. Much of what can be accomplished for the department has to be done through people, and he has to learn to trust his subordinates and delegate more to them. He should watch how well they handle delegated tasks, coach them to correct their mistakes, assess what they have accomplished, and give them more responsibility when warranted. In this way, he will be able to free himself from many operational details and devote his time to more important tasks: to establishing plans and priorities, developing a more effective budget, improving customer relations, purchasing new equipment and supplies, and setting standards of performance appropriate to the unit he manages.

In all this, obviously, you are trying to get across to your boss a philosophy of sound motivational management. The modern manager attempts to multiply himself through his people. The motivation of subordinates and the full utilization of their abilities, ideas, and talents will enable him to look good. At the same time, he has to monitor subordinates to assure that their daily operational performance is satisfactory. When he tries this management philosophy, he will discover that he is taking no greater risks; that he has more time to allot to problems of growth, expansion, and competition; that his people are delivering; and that as they deliver he comes through more effectively to his superiors. He will then have less affinity for the panic button.

Perhaps his superiors can help too. One suggested approach is to spotlight for him the Bureau of the Census' 4:1 figures, which show that there are four times as many widows in our population as there are widowers. The message: many a boss burns himself out well before his time. The panic-button boss, with all the self-induced pressures and tensions, could easily be one of them.

If he follows these guidelines, he will use the panic button only occasionally. He may miss the darn thing. It may rust through disuse. Buy him a new one for his next birthday if he really misses it. Better to laugh with him and through him than at him.

A special note of caution about the proprietor, the man who recites the litany of how much blood, sweat, and tears he shed building the business all by himself. There are no guidelines for dealing with him. He has no interest other than to leave a legacy to his heir. In the early days, his business was a mom-and-pop affair. Though considerably bigger and more prosperous today, it still is a mom-and-pop business — with new characters in the scenario such as sons-in-law and nephews. The "old man" is bent on building a monument to himself, and he doesn't realize how close he is to that vision. There really isn't much you can do about it, except to be sure you send a sympathy card on that sad day.

The Freewheeler

Damn the Choreography:
I'll Do My Own Dance

Background Profile

The freewheeler manager is the business counterpart of Colonel Hogan of the renowned *Hogan's Heroes*. Just as Hogan spends every moment plotting how to get around Sergeant Schultz and Colonel Klink, so the freewheeler boss devotes his time to finding ways to beat the system and the organization.

Working with him is almost an invitation to anarchy. Foremost in his mind is a desire to buck the organization and the system, but he is smart enough to do it with sufficient safeguards. While he is not opposed to the establishment, he is impatient at the restrictiveness of organizational systems. It's just too laborious and slow for him to get a requisition approved, a vacancy filled, a piece of equipment installed, a parking place changed, an adding machine repaired, a new safety feature added, a grievance acted on to his satisfaction, a memo cleared, or a recommendation approved. His mind is spinning with ways to cut corners and get more action. You and other subordinates are in a bind, for you know what is spinning there above his shoulders and will usually nod agreement to his plan even though it runs counter to company ground rules.

To beat the system he has an arsenal of weapons. He will make unholy alliances with those in the company who also have some kind of beef and who can lubricate the wheels for him. He will cut corners and try to get one approval rather than the two required. He is a pretty good politician and will play office politics as often as suits his purpose. He is adept at manipulation but stops short of blackmail. The task of conferring or consulting straightforwardly with others is not to his liking, for it restricts his movement as an individual. He will confer only if really necessary or if he can extract something for future use to his advantage. Reneging on agreements is not difficult for him, for he has learned the art of putting little in writing and of having momentary lapses of memory. Whenever a policy or order is drafted, he immediately requests a series of exceptions. Whether he is in research and development, sales, finance, production, or any other department, his rallying cry is the same: "We're different in our department and it will hurt us badly."

His tactics include pulling surprises, dashing off a memo to someone who is about to leave for an extended trip, twisting the rulebook to make any pretext look like a valid precedent, keeping two sets of files and selecting out the more private contents to foil any after-hours prowler, and pledging his secretary to secrecy. He evades paperwork, fudges on reports, proposes nonsense work for committees to keep them away from his doors, and "cases the joint" before he attends a meeting.

In short, the freewheeler is the organizational maverick. He not only will stand up and oppose a new requirement but will try his artful best to get around it. He is not new to the game of divide and conquer. While careful not to offend any of the still powerful oldtimers in the company, he never ceases his subtle needling of the organizational maze and its intricacies. Very often he succeeds in instituting an organizational change that will give him more latitude—a change slight enough not to bother others but substantial enough to meet his needs. He delights in playing the maverick. Like him or dislike him, he is never dull.

Let's not fault this man, the freewheeler. Many a manager finds himself strapped by archaic and restrictive organizational systems. The freewheeler simply refuses to be boxed in by the intricate network unless there is proof that it contributes to a more efficient operation: to producing a better service, manufacturing a better product, making a sale, or beating a competitor in the industry. Indeed, every organization should be able to tolerate a maverick, a dissenter, as long as the unit he represents is able to measure up to expectations.

Tendencies

The most obvious tendency of the freewheeler boss is risk taking. Along with his bravado, manipulation, and short-circuiting of organizational channels, he takes risks that can jeopardize his reputation and inevitably the reputation of his department. There is always the chance that he will be caught in the act. There is always the likelihood that another boss, who knows of and resents his activities, will "sing" to higher-ups, overtly or anonymously. The hazard is that if the freewheeler boss is caught, the department is caught—the well-being, reputation, and future of employees are at stake. The risks may not always be great, but they are too many and are ventured too often.

In his actions, the freewheeler tends to hinder the work of the management team. Membership on the management team gives him status, but it also makes him somewhat unsteady. He views each new organizational announcement as a great leap backward. At some point negative attitude will impair the loyalty and cohesion of the management team, which is expected to implement newly announced policies and requirements.

In his pursuit of an advance tipoff or an alliance, he tends to handle confidential information too freely. There is always the possibility of leakage of information from the freewheeler. It could be information from a report, a survey, a record, a committee deliberation, or a conversation. Whatever the source, the careless and indiscreet handling of information could lead to distortion, unnecessary feuds, and setbacks to new projects. If he continues the indiscretion after work hours, the information could fall into the hands of a rival company.

This man's attitudes show through. He regards committees as a nuisance, staff advisers as dreamers, quality control experts as intruders, budgetary controls as handcuffs, and administrative assistants as flunkies. To the freewheeler, the annual report is a journalistic coup to dupe stockholders, the settlement with the union is "the great sellout," and coordination is a daily exercise of armtwisting. He knows too well that he must live amicably with the controller, so he soft-pedals his remarks about accounting, computers, and statistical reports. However, he will do battle with the controller too if the issue is important enough.

He has a right to his attitudes regarding the organization. And when it is difficult to work through the formal organization, he can and should tap the underworld of the informal organization to get things done. But when his actions extend beyond that, he could indeed jeopardize the well-being of the department.

The tendency to renege on agreements can contaminate an organization. The questionable ethics of the freewheeler generate distrust, undue caution, and feuds among supervisory and management personnel. Much of the internal business of a company is conducted on the basis of working relationships rather than according to the manual—and the violation of an agreement, an understanding, or a commitment erodes and demoralizes relationships. More important, it can destroy the most vital communication channel in a modern business organization. This is a frightful loss.

For all his subtle and direct protest, the freewheeler boss generally acquits himself well with top management by having his department measure up to expected results. This, he knows, is his insurance policy. With this as a safeguard, he can then embark on risky ventures. Moreover, he doesn't allow organizational restraints to hamper his department more than absoutely necessary. He tends to use the department as an incubation chamber for his own ideas, and now and then he hatches something that is very well received by top management. And his subordinates, though wary of his exploits, are behind him.

Meanwhile, there are many interested spectators watching this man do his tightrope act and subconsciously hoping that he will lose his footing and plunge to the ground below. They are not too solicitous about his recovery.

Analysis

How do we explain the behavior of the freewheeler? First we should distinguish between the freewheeler who manipulates for personal ends and the freewheeler who manipulates for the good of the department. There are freewheeler bosses whose sole motivation is their own advancement, and their techniques are directed to this end. But in most cases the freewheeler is guided by other motives: most of what he does and the direct or devious ways in which he does it is in behalf of the office, the plant, or the department he represents. His intent is to champion the work unit in trying to attain established objectives. That he is obviously impatient, restless, and overeager is another matter.

One school of thought holds that the nonconformist, the maverick, the rebel is always with us—and that's not at all bad.

Others, seasoned observers of the management scene, contend that if companies expect and want innovation they have to give the innovator elbow room and must expect some clash between the desire for organizational stability and the desire for breakthroughs. Those who are freewheelers sometimes give their own explanation: to be a doer, to get results, you have to know the ins and outs and make deals within the company.

The explanations as to what makes our man tick vary. Some psychologists address themselves to the freewheeler's ambivalence: he is a man caught between the desire for two things (conformity and attainment) and trapped into contradictory behavior. Other psychologists interpret the extreme case of the freewheeler as neurotic: he is a man who aggressively resists anything that impedes him. Still others regard him as maladjusted, as an oddball.

Some freewheelers act as they do because of inexperience. In their eagerness to produce results, they seek any means of expediting matters. Others have built their reputations as technical specialists through their own initiative and creativity, with little or no dependency on the organization. Now, as managers, they find it difficult to make the transition from individual effort to organizational conformity and resort to freewheeling as a way out.

Perhaps the most credible explanation is simply this: many bosses are resentful of the administrative process with all its legalisms, complex relationships, waiting periods, and restrictive and unreasonable controls. They oppose the hierarchy of approvals, the meagerness of delegated authority, the retention of unproductive employees, and the distrust that they feel to be inherent in operating procedures. Little wonder that they rebel. If results can be obtained only when things happen, then it may take a little or a lot of freewheeling to *make* things happen.

How to Work With and Help This Boss

It should be evident at the outset that the freewheeler cannot get by with "Damn the choreography, I'll do my own dance." He will need three feet to do the intricate steps and the kind of dancing required in a business enterprise.

Several don'ts for you, the subordinate, in helping the free-wheeler:

☐ Don't be an agent for his plots and machinations. If you act as his emissary or front man and get caught in the dealings, he will probably disclaim ever having known you. If he embarks on a mission — even a somewhat shady mission — that you think will aid the department, nod your approval. Offer a tactical point here and there if you are asked. But don't go out as an espionage agent. The organizational loner will have to go it alone.

☐ Don't be impatient with him. Rest assured that the freewheeler will find a way.

☐ Don't divulge what he's up to. If anyone is to put out feelers or do reconnaissance, he is the one to do it. If he is as good an office politician as he thinks he is, he will do it well, without tipping his hand.

Now for several positive guidelines in trying to help this boss, the freewheeler:

☐ Try to determine just what it is in his background or employment experience that accounts for his insistence on bucking the organization. Just one event, one incident, may have triggered his attitude, and he may still be smarting from the wounds of that incident. He may be obsessed with the need to retaliate. The organization and all it represents is his target in trying to get even.

You may be able to uncover the incident by probing around a bit, or speaking to him in private when he is more talkative. Listen for any inadvertent remark that reveals the scars of that incident. Do it discreetly and in good faith. You may be helping him to unload a burden that he has been carrying for a long time. If you do discover what the incident was, try to open his eyes to the fact it is now history, that he has recouped his losses. Stress to him that if he continues to retaliate he may be hurting himself and the department.

☐ Use your friends and your contacts. It could well be that he is not as antiestablishment as he seems. Harry Truman once advised: "If you can't stand the heat, stay out of the kitchen." In most cases the freewheeler can stand the heat. What he can't stand is the smell.

If you find that he is impatient with bureaucracy, pettiness, and restrictions in other departments, try talking to employees there. Perhaps you can get them to waive a procedure, relax some controls that were once vital but that no longer have importance, communicate with your boss orally rather than in writing, or invite him to go over some interesting plans they have in mind. Whatever you can do to reduce the tensions among departments and bring them together will be all to the good. After all, there are times when a subordinate can and should serve as a goodwill ambassador.

☐ Get him to de-escalate the feuds. Standing up for one's convictions, forcing a confrontation to settle an issue, scoring a point in one's favor—these are understandable. But carrying on feuds, fostering opposition camps, playing good guys and bad guys—these are unproductive in the long run.

☐ Raise some doubts in his mind. He may be too comfortable with his own instincts. Make him uncomfortable now and then by posing some serious questions about the risks the department is taking by embarking on some bold adventure. In being stirred to doubt, he may reveal his own vulnerabilities. This may not be bad at all. It is healthy psychologically to see the need to reveal one's weaknesses. In his case, the one big vulnerability is this: in trying to outsmart others, he may one fine day outsmart himself.

☐ Help him overcome his parochialism. Needle him to accept an appointment to a committee, a task force, a survey group, a troubleshooting team, or other body designated to help the company improve some area of business. Your boss, the freewheeler, may appear to be an adept politician but he may also be afflicted with t.v.—tunnel vision. He can see only the corridor leading to his department and solely what influences the department for better or worse. It makes sense up to a point. It is also an unfortunate form of parochialism.

The best cure for tunnel vision is to develop a broader perspective on the goals and aspirations of the company and to see how managers in other departments view their roles. Getting immersed in activities that go beyond the boundaries of one's department is highly effective therapy. In working with others on a committee or a troubleshooting team the freewheeler may come to realize that there are more common bonds than differences among departments.

☐ Do everything you can to make him more flexible. Try to get him to see his situation realistically. It is a fact of life that the organization is likely to outlive the dissenter. The point is that the individual and the organization should try to accommodate each other to find an acceptable way of resolving corporate, group, and individual differences. This means, of course, that both the organization and the individual have to be willing to bend at times. Business is not a game of winners and losers. The score is of little consequence. What really counts are the figures on the quarterly and annual financial statements, which reflect the company's economic health and its competitive position in the industry.

It is not always a question of *who* is right. More crucial is the question of *what* is right. That is, what will in the long run serve the best organizational and economic interests of the company? And so bending may be better than plotting.

☐ Fight off his isolationism. There is always the danger that in his self-righteous role as the corporate Don Quixote, the freewheeler may be isolating the department. In doing so he may be creating in his department precisely what he abhors in other departments—bureaucracy. An effective boss has to learn the ways of bureaucracy without himself becoming a bureaucrat. Make him aware of this important management strategy, which he probably doesn't have in his little notebook. It is an art that comes with time and experience. In isolating the department, he will hurt himself, his employees, and the department as a whole.

☐ Get him to see the difference between being opportunistic and taking advantage of opportunities. The freewheeler is an opportunist—or at least he appears that way to others. But his luck as an opportunist could run out; it is not guaranteed. If it were, he would do better to leave the company and spend all his time at the racetrack picking horses.

A smart boss will watch for the right opportunity and take advantage of it. This is quite different from being an opportunist. Some of the pointers: know the sources of opportunity in the company, especially during periods of expansion or modernization (and sometimes in periods of contraction as well); cultivate friends and keep building good relationships; work seriously at preparing proposals and develop the self-confidence to make a convincing presentation to upper management; and don't trust to luck. This should be your advice to your boss. This is what differentiates the willful opportunist from the manager who sees and capitalizes on an attractive opportunity. As Louis Pasteur counseled his students: "Luck often follows those who are trained to see the opportunity."

In summary, increased self-awareness, greater empathy, deescalation of feuds, more exposure to working as a member of a team, learning to bend, understanding the ways of bureaucracy so that one can deal with it, learning how to recognize and take advantage of opportunities — these are some of the ways in which the freewheeler can broaden himself as a manager.

A postscript: An organization should be able to tolerate a maverick or loner, even an oddball. However, widespread freewheeling can be the ruination of an organization. Where a number of freewheelers in the company are permitted to go their merry way, top management will soon have to hire a Vice-President in Charge of Intrigue.

The Commandant

"Theirs Not to Reason Why;
Theirs But to Do and Die."

Background Profile

To many a boss, the company is an interlocking network of functions, systems, and people harnessed toward the attainment of economic objectives. To the commandant, however, the company is an entity ever mobilized for combat, and his own department is a battle station. It is *his* battle station, and he is to be in absolute authority. One might believe that after the interview in which he was hired he was not just processed as are ordinary people; he took vows. A kind of military ritualism pervades his paperwork, his appointments, his attendance at meetings — not to mention his orders. Only this kind of distortion of the concept of a business organization (other than some psychological disturbance) would seem to account for the behavior of the commandant.

Everything he does is designed to pay homage to some generalissimo in the company. The commandant hopes that by putting himself in the generalissimo's grace, he too will move up in the ranks. He expects subordinates to knuckle under and to obey orders without question. If this boss had a slogan, it would be the one on the preceding page (from Tennyson's *Charge of the Light Brigade*). To him, policies are supreme edicts — even if they do not make any sense. Procedures are inviolate, and instructions are to be followed to the letter and with haste.

You may recognize the commandant by other names with which he is often tagged, the little Napoleon, the bulldozer, the dictator, the autocrat, the slave driver, the authoritarian. He drives others, but he also drives himself. The compulsion to pay homage to his generalissimo impels him to work harder and longer, with limitless devotion. He becomes a work addict. No task is too much and no requests are too many. He has the chevrons on his sleeve to prove it.

Generally methodical and orderly, the commandant reacts quite emotionally when he is blocked by someone or something: he becomes belligerent; he blusters and threatens. His relationship with subordinates is proper and cordial enough in open quarters, but behind the scenes he is ever pushing, pressuring, and demanding, even when he is not blocked. And when he is displeased with an employee's performance (to him, another form of blockage), intimidation, sarcasm, and threat are the weapons he draws from his arsenal. Well before an employee mishandles an operation, misses a cue, or slows down at a job, this boss will meddle and take over the task himself. As he rolls up his sleeves, you will hear this refrain: "If you want something done right, you have to do it yourself." He is not so much the demanding one as the impatient one.

In his dealings with the generalissimo, the commandant is on his best behavior. He is very frequently a yes-man. Another side of the man shows up in his dealings with subordinates. He becomes domineering, intolerant, driving, at times quick-tempered, threatening, and authoritarian. He will give an employee muttered thanks when a job is well done but will blast the employee with criticism when the job is undone, not done well enough, or not done in time to suit him. He will fume about what the employee did wrong but will not guide him as to how to do it right. When things do not go well on any particular Monday, he will criticize the entire department and find not a grain of good in anyone. It is at this point that he performs his ritual. He retreats to the men's room to reflect, and while washing his hands before the mirror he recites: "Mirror, mirror, on the wall, how do I manage to fire 'em all?"

Again, we see the two sides of the commandant. Male chauvinist, hero worshipper, and adorer of those in the upper echelons of the company, he nevertheless finds it more comforting to surround himself with weak, submissive people. He is driven by a desire to move upward, to beat other managers in the race to promotion and prestige, and he wants to be sure that there will be no mutiny in his ranks while his sights are elsewhere. Moreover, he finds that with so-called weaker people he can continue unabated his ironhanded rule. He derives a glow of power and status from seeing people "lick the dust."

It is essential to distinguish the profile of the commandant from that of the panic-button boss, for there are important differences as well as similarities in their behavior. The commandant is generally well organized and systematic; the panic-button boss is usually disorganized and reacts not to systems but to emergencies and crises. The former is generally more staid;

the latter is more capricious, excitable, and reckless. Both, however, try to run a one-man show, and both create for their people a pressure-cooker environment.

A clarification is in order too in comparing the commandant with the freewheeler boss. The commandant views the organizational structure with reverence and awe, and compliance with organizational requirements is his virtue. In contrast, the freewheeler is a nonconformist who tries to beat the system. Both, however, are power players, both are engaged in rivalries and in trying to outdo others in getting ahead, and both push themselves and their people.

Tendencies

The commandant's behavior as a boss has its impact on the department and on employees. In his distrust of people, his constant supervision of their performance, and his meddling with their jobs, this boss is regarded by his employees with disdain, sometimes with disgust. As a nonlistener, he discourages them from coming forward with ideas and suggestions that could lead to improvements. The department is the loser.

The boss who is out to make his employees knuckle under, who is intent on getting even when he is thwarted, who threatens rather than teaches, who is quick to criticize but slow to commend, who derives some sadistic pleasure in pressuring people with mounting workloads and personal abuse—this boss dare not count on employee loyalty. Their loyalty is to the in-basket and the clock on the wall, and that is as far as it goes. No allegiance is built, surely none that is enduring. He gets about as much loyalty as he gives. Demoralize people and you demoralize whatever dignity there is in work. As Dostoevsky once cautioned: "To make a man feel worthless, keep him at work that is meaningless." Prison wardens have long been expert at this.

His department registers higher turnover rates than other departments, and the costs, direct and indirect, are frightfully high. People with self-respect and ability will tolerate the commandant up to a certain point. After that they get busy typing and distributing their résumés. A good taker comes along and they are gone. Disdainful of people, the commandant will nevertheless reach into his budget and add more employees to compensate for the depressed motivation and limited productivity of those already on the payroll. To some extent, this tactic is also a conscious effort at empire building. The bigger the department, the more people at his command—and the greater the feeling of power for the commandant.

When the climate is such that employees are fearful of making an error, it is unlikely that they will accept delegated tasks, no matter what authority the boss has. All a subordinate has to do is to bungle a delegated task once and he will not be called upon in the future. The task is returned to the commandant's desk. At this point subordinates begin to wonder who is working for whom. They become reluctant or unwilling to take on delegations. The reasons they give are legion and quite imaginative. Basically, they will not be victimized by his impatience, meddling, sarcasm, and premature withdrawal of a task entrusted to them. So better not even to begin. The commandant is then compelled to add to his own overload of work as the head of the department, and his addiction to work continues unabated.

Now and then he tends to pick his own cabinet of advisers to give him a hand. They are usually the same submissive yes-men who make him comfortable but offer no relief. They are not likely to make any critical contribution to the commandant's problem-solving or decision-making abilities.

Unable to cope effectively with the dynamics of interpersonal and group relations, this boss resorts to structural changes. Structure does not talk back. Thus he is driven to reorganizing and making clean sweeps of his department. In time, his subordinates become accustomed to the game of musical chairs; they view him as a reorganization-happy manager and see all his ventures as just so much spinning of wheels. He will not tolerate employee resistance to change. Changes are not merely made; they are decreed. But many of these changes run into conflict with psychological barriers to acceptance and are subtly ignored or quietly sabotaged. True, structure does not talk back—it backfires.

The commandant's tendency to play vassal to the lord often makes him look ludicrous. He is regarded as a courier of messages rather than as a manager. Devotion to the generalissimo forces him to play the role of courier. For all his domineering, pressuring, blustering, and threats, subordinates see him as a little man, a managerial Faust.

Within the company, rivalries tend to become tainted. Just as the commandant regards other men as threats in the race for promotion, so they come to see him as a threat. They are alert to his tradeoffs, the cliques that he courts, his secret meetings with the generalissimo, and the build-up of employee resentment over his pressure tactics and his bullying. They construct dossiers. They develop their own network of wiretaps to obtain confidential information about the commandant. In short, the contestants in the race to get ahead become rivals, the rivals become corporate enemies, and sooner or later an enemy will cut the commandant down to size.

Finally, there is a very real danger that the commandant's authoritarian values and methods will spread to others in the department. If and when contagion makes departmental dictatorship an accepted way of life for managers and supervisors, the company will have taken a giant leap backward. There are enough latent dictators around. Let us not put them in a position to command responsibility over others—not in the political community *or* in the business community.

Analysis

How do we explain the behavior of the commandant—the despot, the authoritarian, the driver, the man intent on pushing people around? We could simply write him off as a manifestation of the sheer brute in man, an example of man's arrogance of power and his abuse of authority. But analysts are having a field day with theories about the behavior of this boss, and they deserve equal time on the air. Here are some of their explanations of what makes the commandant tick.

Some analysts point to the fact that he derives strength and power by surrounding himself with weaker people, and this is sufficiently ego-fulfilling. Others maintain that he needs to find a scapegoat either to unload his feelings of guilt, whatever their source, or to reinforce and sustain his desire for dominance. In this he will deprecate not only submissive employees but also those who have qualities that he lacks and therefore resents: better education, higher intelligence, greater creativity. It should not be surprising that some analysts return to the theory that this boss thrives on following in the footsteps of an aggressive, demanding father. Dad was also somewhat of a brute but was worshipped by his son, later to become the commandant.

Other analysts hold that the commandant's behavior is a dramatic overcompensation for his rejection somewhere in the past as a softy. Indeed, in his kowtowing to the generalissimo in upper management he is punishing himself for the softness or humaneness he showed in the past. The gnawing desire to surpass someone, if he cannot surpass something, is another explanation of his race with others for promotion.

Insecurity, especially as exhibited in his distrust of subordinates and in his fear that someone will try to take his job, may also explain the commandant's need for absolute control. Perhaps this apparent authoritarian is just a little man so wrapped up in himself and his own interests that he is unable to reach out to others. One provocative theory explains the commandant's behavior in these terms: deprived of other forms of power—social power, economic power, creative power, or even sexual power—he seeks power over others to compensate for what he lacks.

Finally, we cannot ignore this straightforward explanation: (1) the commandant dupes himself into believing that he is a leader who generates some kind of magnetism in the department, yet all he really generates is pressure; (2) very much like the nice-guy manager, but at the other pole, he confuses the concept of toughness with tough-mindedness; and (3) the only reason he gets away with his authoritarian behavior is that someone higher up in the company lets him get away with it. Two brutes have quietly made a pact to support each other at the expense of the human resources of the organization.

Before we decide to cast this fellow to the sharks, let's pause for a moment to reflect on his behavior. There is something to be said in behalf of the commandant. He is dedicated and loyal to the company; he is a devoted and tireless worker. He has a good perspective of what is expected of a middle manager or a supervisor. That is, he recognizes that his principal responsibility is upward: it is his job to understand the goals and timetables of top management and to work toward achieving these goals. He knows that his main role is to implement and follow up on policies, programs, projects, and special assignments. He can be looked upon favorably as among those bosses who are thinking of next year's profits. He does get results. In these respects, he leads from some strengths.

His weaknesses lie in the methods by which he goes about getting results: in his desire to make people cringe, in his distrust, in his abuse of authority, in his blind obedience, in his underutilization of human talent. He is downright ignorant of the larger understanding of motivation in human relations. And he is a fool to believe that he can run roughshod over people without paying for it in the end. The day of reckoning will come, and the irony is that he will himself accelerate the coming.

Enough of psychological analyses and of moralizing. Let's proceed with what can be done positively in trying to manage the commandant.

How to Work With and Help This Boss

First a series of don'ts for you, the subordinate, in dealing with the commandant:

☐ Don't do anything to impair his initiative, his desire for action and results. Whatever you may think of him personally, the fact is that the department needs this momentum.

☐ Don't take him by surprise with bad news. He doesn't relish the idea of going to the generalissimo with problems. Try to anticipate any difficulties that may arise and do what you can to head them off or let him know about them well in advance.

☐ Don't give him a bum steer. He has already developed a distrustful attitude toward people, and this may only intensify his attitude. Moreover, if you do give him a bum steer, he may well believe that you have been planted by the enemy as a fifth column to sabotage his operations.

☐ Don't try one-upmanship on him. It could cost you dearly. The line between abuse of power and outright hostility is a very thin one indeed. Any attempt at one-upmanship would be a frightful blow to his ego. So if you want to chance it, be prepared to resign if it backfires.

☐ Don't try to make inroads by getting into informal, off-the-record chats with him. It's a waste of time, because he can't stand openness.

☐ Don't expect him to become gentle. If he knew that his promotion depended on his ability to work better with people, he might modify his behavior. But he will never become really humane.

With this set of don'ts, where do you go from here in your relationship with the commandant? Do you capitulate—grin and bear it, letting him have his way? Do you wait it out? A successor may come along shortly. Do you call it quits when you've had enough of him and pursue your career elsewhere? Do you try to help him manage more effectively *without* pushing people around and abusing authority?

You may decide on any one of these tactics, depending upon your patience, the degree of self-respect you have retained, the state of your health, how badly you need the job, the extent to which you have been stymied, your sense of forgiveness and compassion, and the kind of inside information you have about the future of your boss.

Apart from any personal decision you may make, let us proceed with the last item in the list: how the commandant might be helped. Here are several guidelines for helping this boss:

☐ Let him know that he is ineffective at working with people, without expressly telling him so. Gather data on the cost to the department of employee turnover, absenteeism, grievances, and lowered productivity because of lowered morale.

Sentiment may not impress him, but cost data and other statistics on the effects of a poor human relations climate might cause him to think. Remind him that the department has lost a number of excellent employees and has never been able to replace them with people of the same caliber. Keep needling him with the names of those who left. Specifics have more impact than generalities.

☐ Seize upon every instance of depressed morale in the department and confront him with it. Have the backbone to level with him as to the cause of the latest decline in morale. Pinpoint where it began. He'll get the message—particularly if the drop in morale has resulted in a significant increase in absenteeism and lowered production in the department.

☐ Try to get to the source of his problem, to find some clue as to why he feels the way he does toward subordinates. See if you can uncover some tangible experiences that account for his distrust of people. Don't write it off as part of his nature. Look for specific incidents and events in the past that might have left him with scars.

☐ Cite other departments in which cooperation rather than fear prevails. You might in time get across the point that undue fear is harmful—and quite unnecessary. There are better ways to obtain the cooperation and responsiveness of subordinates.

☐ When he keeps talking of how well the company treats its people in terms of money and fringe benefits, remind him of those who left because they wanted more than money. Monetary reward is important, no doubt, but people also want to know they are valued as people—with minds, abilities, and aspirations. Employees who get no cue now and then that their services are valued feel themselves to be of little or no worth. Their morale and productivity suffer.

☐ Set him straight on what motivating employees really means. At times he may lapse into a state of "real concern for our people" and may toss the word "motivation" around freely. If he has just come back from a management seminar, he may even be brazen enough to mention Maslow, McGregor, or Herzberg to support his use of the term. You would do well to go him one better and drop him a memo with this quote from

Robert Townsend's *Up the Organization:* "You can't motivate people. You *can* create a climate in which most of your people will motivate themselves to help the company reach its objectives."[1] He might think well enough of the quote to slip it under his desk blotter and look at it now and then when no one is around.

There is a good body of evidence that a positive approach to management is one in which the manager gets people to do what he wants through establishing goals, setting an example, developing a climate in which self-motivation can thrive, and valuing subordinates for their contribution to the department. A manager who takes such an approach will find that in the process he too is growing.

☐ Counteract his incessant demands, orders, and criticisms by insisting on the formulation of work standards. If he is slow about getting to this task, then work with others to draft a set of acceptable performance standards for each job in the department. Such a scorecard will enable him to judge whether a man is exceeding the standards, just meeting the standards acceptably, or falling below the standards of performance. He can then direct his criticisms and threats more meaningfully to the few rather than the many. This should at least reduce the volume of abuse hurled by the commandant.

If the standards seem fair and attainable and are acceptable to both management and employees, do not let him unilaterally scrap them and return to purely subjective judgments. Do battle with him to restore the standards of performance; raise the issue with top management if necessary. If the union is willing to support you, accept this additional muscle to do battle. There may be some bloody noses, but the chances are good that you will win the battle of the standards.

☐ Chip away at his emphasis on toughness — physical toughness — in getting results. At the same time, get him to see the difference between toughness and tough-mindedness in management. More about this later.

☐ Alter his stand regarding mistakes. Show him that people can

[1] Robert Townsend, *Up the Organization* (New York: Knopf, 1970), p. 142.

both recover from and learn from mistakes. Yet try to make your own performance as blameless as possible. No one is infallible, not even the commandant, and he knows it but keeps it quiet. Get to mistakes promptly and do your best to correct them.

☐ Haggle with him over any special projects or assignments he wants to delegate to you. Show your displeasure in having him second-guess you and prematurely break in on your assigned task. Make him promise to stay out of it and to check with you only occasionally. Stress the end result of the delegation — what you can show him as the finished product.

☐ Report to him regularly and on time, following established reporting practice in the department. Nothing shakes him up more than failure to comply with procedure. This shatters the ritual. You'll have to get to the report eventually, so you might as well do it on time, do it well, and have it ready when he asks for it. If for some good reason you are unable to report on schedule, check with him in advance.

☐ Make every effort to do your best when he is away — at home with the flu, on a trip, on vacation, and so on. In time he may come to realize that his people are capable of performing effectively on the job not only without fear and intimidation but even without his presence.

☐ Keep him honest. When he comes back from the generalissimo's office with a new order, a veto of a request, a budget cut, or some other message, quiz him sufficiently to make sure that it is not a ruse. The message may be entirely his own doing and may not have come from the generalissimo at all. If you don't keep him honest, he will continue to mount more pressures, real or disguised.

☐ If the occasion arises when he appears willing to open up and to be receptive to suggestions, take advantage of the opportunity. Level with him. Point out that there is no great virtue in working harder when he could be working smarter, and that the smart way is to tap the capabilities and energies of subordinates without coercion or pressure. Let him know that his emotions sometimes get in the way of his judgment, so suggest that he count to ten before letting go with a blast of criticism, and remind him of specific times when he exploded at employees without knowing the full story.

Make him aware of the fact that he might have less difficulty making changes if he tried to install some changes on an experimental basis. Remind him that good self-control leads to effective control of others. Do it diplomatically, but do it. You will not have such an opportunity again for some time. All this adds up to a most important point that every boss should understand: there is often a large gap between how a manager perceives himself as a boss and how others perceive him. This may not be any news to him, but it may prompt him to narrow the gap a little.

☐ Recognize that any efforts at improving communication will have to flow primarily one way—from you and other employees to him. In his mind, communication from him to you means commands, instructions, and requests from the battle station. This is clearly restrictive communication. So be prepared to carry the brunt of initiating communications that have to do with ideas, work situations, proposals, problems, morale, incentives, and so on. Only then will you be able to establish a true interchange of ideas—when he *has* to respond to your suggestions for his own welfare and that of the department. After all, it's no surprise: he is as ineffective at communicating as he is at dealing with people.

☐ Get across to him the concept of management by exception. As a boss, he should get involved mainly in extraordinary or urgent matters—problems that cannot be handled adequately at the employee level—and should refrain from becoming involved in day-to-day operational activities that employees are quite capable of handling themselves. Persuade him that this will ease his workload and save much of his energy.

☐ Insist on a hearing when he turns down an idea that you and others consider valuable to the department. Pin him down to justify his rejection. If he refuses to give any explanation, join forces with your co-workers to find ways of retaliating and of showing your discontent. Keep a record of the incident—the idea, the date, the rejection, the failure to explain, the expressed resentment. Throw it at him the next time he gives a pep talk on the need for good suggestions. It will be a more telling blow.

☐ Capitalize on his fears. Even the little dictator is afraid. The commandant is plagued by the fear that he will miss out on the cherished promotion — even after all the dedication, the friendship with the generalissimo, the incessant work, the politicking, and the self-denial. He knows that a company could withhold a promotion for any reason. Any grievance, any mistake, any leak, any whim of the appointing officers could knock him out of the running. Take advantage of this fear.

Make him aware that one of the things that may be holding him back is his domineering treatment of people. Let him know that word gets around to other departments and from other departments to higher-ups, and that this could endanger his chances for promotion. He may well decide to trade off his brutal instincts for an opportunity to get ahead. You may see some change in his usual behavior.

In his article "The Promotion Illusion," a study of what puts men in the running for promotion, Thomas Zimmer lists eight criteria that business managers rely on in sizing up the "most promotable" employees. The top three criteria are: (1) ability to make decisions, (2) effectiveness in working with people, and (3) ability to develop subordinates. By these standards, it would seem that the commandant fulfills only a third of the requirements for promotion.[2]

It has been said that every boss with any aspirations has to keep his eyes on three jobs: the job above his (his boss's job), which he must learn; the job he holds, which he must do well; and the job below his, which he must teach. The commandant may have to work harder at his own job and at the task of teaching others if he is to have any hope of obtaining the job above.

Moreover, such factors as growth, diversification, competition, and new technology make continuing self-development as a manager essential. A manager must be able to learn new skills or competencies and to unlearn some of his old skills and habits. Unless you help him to help himself, the commandant may have quite a time unlearning his old habits of pressuring people and dominating them unnecessarily.

[2] Thomas Zimmer, "The Promotion Illusion," *Management of Personnel Quarterly* (Winter 1970), pp. 8–16.

Special Focus

Several subjects warrant special focus in regard to the commandant and your efforts to make him look good.

First, as to the distinction between drive and the driver. What businesses seek in a manager is drive. A manager with drive has a desire to improve, to change, to innovate. He is concerned with moving toward established objectives, purposes, and goals; he is restless with the status quo. He is able to see new vistas and to join together with others to solve an unusual problem or to meet an emergency.

In contrast, the driver is one who physically and emotionally drives himself and others. He pushes people around, threatens them, and exerts pressures to make it clear that he is to have his way and that they are to make it so. It is sad that companies tolerate the drivers. It is encouraging that few companies either mandate them or sanction them.

Drive is an enduring asset to a company. Drivers, however, come and go. They go when the company discovers that it is paying too high a price for the results they attain. Or they go when competing managers find some skeletons in the closet of the drivers and blackmail them. There is, then, the boss who breaks doors down and pushes people around, and there is the boss who pulls himself and his people together—who works quietly, purposively, and decently and who gets a helluva lot done. There may be a lesson in this for you as you work with the commandant.

Second, as to authority and its distortion and abuse. There are different kinds of authority in business: authority that comes with the status of a given organizational position; authority that stems from knowledge, experience, and special competency; authority that comes with distinguished accomplishment; authority that springs from the influence of the informal organization given to its spokesman; authority that comes with creative, innovative ideas; and authority derived from character and example which evoke the respect of others. The commandant can lay claim only to the first type of authority. He has only the authority conferred on him by his payroll title as boss—and the support given him by the generalissimo. He has the trappings and the symbols of organizational authority. But he has yet to earn authority in the eyes of others.

Moreover, in business a manager rarely has complete, absolute authority. At any give time, he has delegated authority, partial authority, authority subject to review, coordinative authority, special authority in an emergency situation, and even seized authority when the responsibility for a task is ambiguous and no one else claims it. The commandant has only the authority accorded him by his position, and even that is limited. So his reckless use or abuse of authority in intimidating people is and should be subject to challenge.

The problem of abuse of authority is summed up well by Peter Drucker in his *Landmarks of Tomorrow:*

> It makes no difference whether abuse of the manager's inherent power is hidden or in the open, whether it is brute oppression or affable manipulation of consent. Nor does it matter whether the motives are selfish or genuine altruism, desire for self-aggrandizement or mistaken kindness. It is abuse, if not despotism, for a manager to aim at power rather than at responsible performance.
>
> The manager has a responsibility to the people working with him. He has the responsibility to build the structure in which men can achieve the most, and to find the right spot in that structure for each of the [employees]. He must make most effective whatever skill and knowledge the specialists have, and give full scope to their judgment. He has to keep them informed of the common goal toward which their efforts are to be directed; and he has to keep himself informed of the new potentials of contribution and performance opened up by advances in areas of specialized knowledge. He has the responsibility to create, in other words, the conditions in which [employees] can both achieve the most and develop themselves the most. And he has the responsibility—both to the individual and to the organization—to demand superior performance and to condone nothing less.[3]

This is a quote worthy of being read and reread by you and especially by your boss.

[3] Peter F. Drucker, *Landmarks of Tomorrow* (New York: Harper & Row, 1959), pp. 79–80.

Third, as to the matter of demanding employee loyalty. Every subordinate has multiple loyalties. He has a loyalty to his profession or trade, a loyalty to the company with which he is affiliated, a loyalty to his immediate boss, a loyalty to his co-workers, and a loyalty to himself—to his aspirations and career goals—and to his family. There is always an interplay among these loyalties, and the way a man responds to a given situation will depend on how he perceives the relative strength of his different loyalties at that particular time. But unquestioning, blind loyalty has no place in a business organization. A business enterprise is not the U.S. Marine Corps or a college alumni association.

The commandant's pressure, intimidation, and incessant demands for performance get results—at a price. They do not get loyalty. The few exceptions are those employees who associate squirming and blind obedience with organizational loyalty.

Fourth, as to the difference between toughness and tough-mindedness. The tough manager is one who is harsh, threatening, iron-handed, and indifferent to the feelings of others. The tough-minded manager is one who has high expectations and who calls for high standards of work performance. He is concerned with employees' will to work and with the quality of their output. He is unwilling to accept a shabby product, a mediocre performance, a late report, an unrealistic schedule, a weak procedure, or a superficial presentation. The tough-minded manager emphasizes the importance of developing realistic goals and targets toward which the energies and talents of subordinates can be directed. And he is candid in letting people know from time to time where they are strong, where they are weak, and how they can overcome some of their weaknesses. In all this, his concern is to level with employees, not to threaten them.

Tough-mindedness will elicit better results than will toughness —and at a price that the company can afford to pay.

Finally, as to the way a manager should give criticism if criticism is called for. To be effective, criticism must be diagnostic and educational. Here is a brief catechism of effective criticism for the manager: choose the right time and place for it and speak calmly; make clear your interest in the employee and in his performance; put the error or fault right on the line, without vagueness; explain the consequences of this kind of error; focus the criticism more on the act than on the person (he'll get the point anyway); be specific about the remedy and be open to other possible remedies to prevent a repeat of the error; let the employee do some talking to explain what he believes to be some of the causes; don't demolish his self-confidence; and get on with the show.

Your task is to help this boss, the commandant, move away from visceral management to rational management — for his good and for the good of the company.

The Mobile Manager

A Man in a Hurry

Background Profile

People select and set their career goals in different ways. One man opts to dedicate himself to a company for a long span of years, perhaps all his adult life. He sees himself as a one-company man. His concern is with security. He seeks slow but definite movement within the company from stock clerk to inventory supervisor to purchasing agent to procurement manager. Ultimate retirement is his reward for many years of loyal service to the company.

Another man finds himself in and out of management jobs, as he is buffeted by the winds of good or bad luck and as opportunities come and go. This will occur, for example, as the aircraft company with which he is affiliated falls heir to an attractive government contract, as the small business enterprise he joined folds because it cannnot stand up against the severe competition, as a new product for which he is sales manager is launched and the market for it booms, or as a merger is effected and in the organizational shuffle he comes out a casualty.

Still another man, the mobile manager, sets for himself a pattern of job hopping as a business career. His life style is characterized by the investment of a few intensive years with Company A, followed by a block of years with Company B, and then an intensive stint with Company C. He seeks to get ahead within or outside the industry, wherever good opportunities arise. His aspirations are different from those of the one-company man. He hopes to show, in time, a string of successful supervisory and management ventures in various reputable companies and to "make it big" by the time he is 40.

Tendencies

Several tendencies are associated with the mobile manager, the man in a hurry. They range from personal behavior and attitudes to responsiveness to corporate pressures.

There is a tendency for the mobile manager to seek assignments, responsibilities, and special projects that offer high visibility. Plainly, he is seeking attention from those in the higher management echelons. Obtaining early recognition is important to the mobile manager, and he constantly strives to be in the spotlight. In his race between demonstrated performance and time, there is no time to be lost.

He is at the same time aware that, because of this visibility, each assignment is critical. As a consequence, he tends to be very demanding of himself and of his people to assure as many successes and as few failures as possible in these special responsibilities or project assignments.

The mobile manager has a tendency to seek the loci of influence, the power centers, in the company. He reads cues, watches his superiors' styles of management, develops a sensitivity to company protocol, and looks for models of managerial behavior that bring rewards. He also sizes up the competition by observing his fellow managers. The mobile manager is often considered an office politician by his co-workers. To the extent that he *can* gain favor and entrée to those in influence or power, he will do so. Being "in favor" is part of his strategy of being successful. He will court such favor but will do so with discretion and good timing. In short, he is willing to win friends who can influence his growth and recognition in the company, but he still wants to build in safeguards to assure that he will remain his own man.

Perhaps the most notable tendency of the mobile manager is his strong desire to achieve. He derives great satisfaction from his accomplishments, and for this reason he gives little margin for mistakes—on either his own part or that of his peers and subordinates. What often appears to others as impersonality on the part of the mobile manager might be better termed a tendency to depersonalize. He is more concerned with action, performance, standards, results, and task achievement than with the personalities, temperaments, and frailties of the people involved. He tends to be especially hard on those whom he has assessed as mental duds, has-beens, slow movers, or petty bureaucrats. This often brings him a label he does not seek—a perfectionist.

Quite early in his tenure on the job the mobile manager shows a tendency to seek more and more logistical support. He presses for more staff, more facilities, a larger budget allocation, more space, more modernized services, and so forth. He is perceptive in recognizing that more resources are the key to potential success in managerial performance.

In his zest for making the most commendable showing in the shortest possible time, the mobile manager often tries to grab total credit. This lapse in acknowledging credit to other colleagues is more than just forgetfulness. It is a breach of ethics to which this manager is particularly susceptible.

There is no doubt that the mobile manager puts his career on the line each time he stretches for new and tougher responsibilities and, correspondingly, for more recognition. This is the risk inherent in his ways. Whether he is more interested in his career than in his company is a moot point. The two, career and company, are probably inseparable in the sense that the result — improved managerial performance and growth — will benefit both the company and himself.

Analysis

In his life style — job-hopping and relocation — the mobile manager clearly takes professional and economic risks, as well as the personal risks that come with being a husband and father. But this should not necessarily make him a target for disdain. After all, his way of life is part of the Protestant success ethic that this country has nurtured since colonial days. The craving for success is an American cult. The eminent researcher in executive mobility, Eugene Jennings, has written extensively on this subject, and his studies show that mobile managers are found in every type of industry as they track their own success records.[1] Indeed, many corporations have insisted on varied experience as a requisite for moving ahead. Moreover, mobility becomes more difficult for the manager after he reaches 40, and he and others know it well. In essence, the behavior of the mobile manager is not so much a case of restlessness or instability as it is an acknowledged part of

[1] See Eugene E. Jennings, *The Mobile Manager* (New York: McGraw-Hill, 1967).

the highway system of routes to business success. Some in our culture prefer to travel this route.

Consequently, let's not stereotype or prejudge the mobile manager. In some instances, he may be a pushy, greedy, sinister character bent on acquiring power. In most instances, however, his movements are on the up and up, and he is determined to give his very best to the company in a few concentrated years and to prove his capabilities to the utmost—despite the ulcers that may develop from his high-intensity input.

How to Work With and Help This Boss

Your boss may well be one of this nomadic tribe, a mobile manager. Here are three important don'ts for you as his aide, secretary, deputy, senior employee, or lower-echelon supervisor:

☐ Don't second-guess the decision of higher-ups to put him on the payroll. They have already sized him up, put him through the wringer, and checked with his former employers and colleagues; they have assessed him as a potential winner, as someone who can make a worthwhile contribution to the company. So try not to question this decision.

☐ Don't ally yourself with those who are deeply sympathetic with the insider who was passed over to make room for the newcomer. Feel sorry for the guy who was hurt by the mobile manager—commiserate with him over several martinis at Pete's Bar and Grill, be philosophical about such events, balm his feelings of distress. But don't fall in with the camp of brothers mourning for one of their kin who was the victim of a "raw deal." If you do ally yourself with this camp and if the followers try openly or covertly to sabotage the new man, you'll be counted among the saboteurs. It is not worth the risk.

☐ Don't question prematurely the loyalty of the mobile manager because he may be with the company only a short time. Just wait and see.

Here is what you can do on the positive side to help this boss:

☐ Help him to learn the ropes as early as possible in the organization. In particular, alert him to where bureaucratic hurdles are to be found and show him how they can be vaulted without stumbling or falling on his face.

☐ Recognize that if he is really a self-starter, a fast learner, and a person who gets results, he can probably accomplish more for the department and for the company (and, of course, for himself) in the short tenure of two to three years than a less capable manager could do in five to six years. So get ready for faster tempo and pace yourself accordingly. You cannot help much by holding to the former pace.

☐ Recognize that as a man in a hurry he has acquired broad exposure from his relatively short stays in other companies. He may have picked up a number of good ideas along the way. He has probably learned the art of cultivating and maintaining good working relationships with fellow managers—an art that he knows to be more important than technical skills. He may put much of this to good use in your department. And better interdepartmental relationships may be just what your department needs most.

☐ Keep abreast of the latest developments in your technical or professional field. He will depend largely on your expertise, rather than on his own. Do not allow yourself to go stale, for rapid advances and changes in a technical field can soon outdistance the practitioner.

☐ Solve as many of the problems at your level as you can. Avoid dumping problems on his desk. His in-basket is probably piled high enough. Do not add to it if possible. Give him some relief.

☐ Make yourself available. Manage your time wisely so that you can be available when he needs you. Avoid becoming overcommitted to projects or encumbered with paperwork. The man in a hurry will generally have a backlog of ideas that he would like to execute, and he will want to delegate a number of special assignments to you and others. He can and will reserve some projects for himself, but he will have to count on subordinates to take on other tasks. Try not to get trapped into a lot of nonsense activities that do not really contribute to the good of the business. When you anticipate that certain commitments will cut deeply into your time, don't make those commitments until you have checked with him. He will then have a better understanding of the extent of your availability.

☐ Participate willingly in working on the blueprint for the future of the department. After his orientation period of a few weeks, he will probably have drafted a statement of how he views the future of the department and what he believes can and should be done. He may or may not have tested out his views with higher-ups; he probably has not yet discussed them with his peers. In all likelihood, he will first want to review a draft statement with you and others in the department. Listen carefully to the objectives, plans, and priorities he has formulated. Mull them over for a few days before you start to nitpick. Then help in the all-important task of giving realism and articulation to the objectives, plans, and priorities: help him to modify, amend, or restate them; recommend some to be dropped and others to be added; and help him to set realistic timetables. Your participation will make it easier for him to present the statement to his superiors for their approval.

☐ Toughen your skin and be ready to take some criticism—not of yourself but of the department. In addition to his blueprint for the future, he will have drafted a critique of the department, its work, and its contribution to the corporate good. Some of his views may be moderately or severely critical of the department. They will threaten your ego, but don't be hypersensitive. The department may have been in the hands of a mediocre nice-guy manager for some time, or it may have been in a rut of routine. If you believe his critique to be valid, support him fully. If you feel that some of the criticisms are cursory or poorly founded, take issue objectively and point out certain facts that he may have overlooked or not understood well enough. This is a meeting of minds, not an arena of battle. He probably wants to know not only how you feel about the critique of the department but also how you think and react—how you view new or different concepts, how you react under stress, and what you do or do not believe regarding management of this unit.

☐ Let him know, candidly, when you are becoming overloaded with work as a result of the new ideas and changes or the faster tempo he has initiated. He won't know if you do not tell him. From that point you will have to level with him as to the impact of the overload and the risks it poses to the quality of work and the morale of the department. He may have to consider adding temporary or permanent staff, restructuring his budget, putting certain priorities on the shelf so you can concentrate on higher-priority activities, or otherwise achieving a sound balance between manpower and workloads. If you are unable to persuade him the first time, try again.

☐ Back off now and then to evaluate what and how well the department is doing. Reports are only one means of control. Face-to-face discussion of "how we're doing" is equally important in management control and evaluation. You can provide for this only by pausing now and then to evaluate, and he expects this of you despite the fast pace of things. Help him to take advantage of the informal network of communication within your department.

☐ As a pro in management, he is astute enough to know that there are always underground channels of communication within the formal organization. It may be a group, a clique, or an informal bond holding people together in the work setting. Informal communication takes place in the car pool, the cafeteria, the men's room, and many other sites.

Since he knows the extent to which the informal organization can contribute to the well-being of the formal organization, the mobile manager will probably reach out to you as a member of or spokesman for the informal group. This is his way of saying that he recognizes the value of the informal group: its ability to help implement a policy on a timely basis, to see that a new change goes through effectively, to make sure that rules are observed, to assist in reallocating work assignments, or to utilize the talents of its people fully and productively. Take his offered hand. He'll need it. If the informal organization proves to be hostile or to operate against the good of the department and the company, he may later try to shake it up—but not break it up. He knows too well that the informal organization cannot be liquidated. All this falls under the general heading of group dynamics—what makes an organization tick.

More Profiles:
THE
DEAD-ENDERS

MORE PROFILES: THE DEAD-ENDERS

A foreword is in order before we proceed to the last three profiles. There are several significant reasons for this. First, in terms of their number this group of bosses exceeds by far all the nice guys, the panic-button pushers, the freewheelers, the commandants, and the mobile managers. Their number is large indeed, and no one is ever likely to know just how many there are. Very many companies would like to keep it a secret. These bosses are the ones who are most often passed up, isolated, written off as has-beens, or otherwise regarded as men who have hit their peak and have no further potential for growth. They are dead-enders, as deemed by their companies. They are neither good enough to be advanced nor poor enough to be fired. So they sit in limbo. Yet many of them are in their 40s or 50s, with 15 years or more to go before they retire. Some are even younger.

Second, the dead-enders not only stifle their own progress; they also block the advancement of others. Younger, more aspiring managers would like to move up in the organization. They want to give evidence of their abilities and talents and to have an opportunity to grow. They cannot move up to the next rung of the ladder when somebody is frozen there. The chain reaction caused by the dead-ender can be very costly to a company in terms of the unused latent abilities of its manpower.

Third, there is a marked apathy, bitterness, insecurity, and even aimlessness among them. Again, this sets in motion a chain reaction. The demoralization spreads to others who work with them. After a while, in their insecurity, they find themselves putting more emphasis on façades and methods of saving face than on maintaining their self-respect.

Fourth, the apathy and staleness of the dead-enders threaten the future of their departments for the next 10 to 15 years. The man and the department he leads are inseparable, and if the man is written off then the department may also be doomed to routine.

For these reasons—the large number involved, the stagnation and underutilization of subordinates, the diminished productivity and morale of the work group, and the threat to the future of the department—the dead-enders merit very serious attention. But are they really dead-enders—men who have reached the peak of their abilities? Or have circumstances within the organization relegated them to a status of being dead-ended? Either may be true. Are they really ineffectual and unproductive as bosses, with no further potential to improve? Or are they just limited, with abilities that can be enlarged given the will, the right climate of encouragement, and some help? Again, either may be true. (If at this point the reader is just itching to cite the Peter Principle, just hold off for a while. This problem of the waste of human lives and human resources is too serious to be dismissed with a formula. More about this later.)

Perhaps the dead-enders are being written off too soon. Their superiors may be too biased or hasty in their judgments. Samuel Johnson, in hearing of a setback of this kind experienced by a friend, responded: "God Almighty, sir, does not propose to judge a man until the *end* of his days." If we were to apply the criteria for failure in business to other sectors of society, we would have to include as failures, at some point in their lives, such men as St. Francis, Jonas Salk, Winston Churchill, Vincent Van Gogh, Robert Taft, Billy Mitchell, and Thomas Edison.

In any event, whether the dead-ender's incompetency is real or alleged, the price the company pays for it is high. The dead-ender's worn-out approaches and sterile viewpoints mean diminished productivity in the department, waste of human resources, and possible decline in the competitive position of the company. The dead-ender is unable to keep pace with company growth, to adapt to new tools for decision making, and to take on new assignments as a boss. He is unable to recognize and take advantage of good opportunities. As a result of his mismanagement of the department, subordinates are blocked and frustrated, and there is a very real danger that they will leave the company and pursue their careers elsewhere.

The need to take action is abundantly clear. Perhaps in your own way you can do something about it in your company.

To close this foreword on a note of optimism, let us advance the hypothesis that the abilities of these bosses — viewed by higher-ups as mediocre, limited, or inadequate — could be expanded with the company's help and with yours. Stretch their capabilities, and American business could gain thousands of man-days of productive management that now go untapped.

The Petty Bureaucrat

Worshipping the System

Background Profile

Communicating with the bureaucratic boss is an ordeal. Many a petty bureaucrat is guided by this formula in regard to communication: when sure, flip to the precise page and paragraph in the manual; when in doubt, mumble.

The petty bureaucrat perceives the company not as an organization but as a place of worship. Company policies are scripture; procedures and methods are rituals. To deviate the least bit from them is to commit sacrilege. He runs the department as though he were a member of a corporate priesthood. In lieu of purple cloths, however, he drapes his department in red tape.

Whether he is attached to the purchasing function, personnel, shipping, accounting, contracting, or building maintenance, this boss is easily recognized. You can't miss him. He lives by the book. Nothing is cleared, nothing is approved, nothing is initialed, and nothing moves unless it fulfills every requirement to the letter. He makes a fetish of paperwork and even casts a spell around it to hoodwink the innocent. His office is ringed with files. The more paperwork, the more people, and soon he will have a nice little empire. Whatever the flow of paper or activity, things get stalled at his desk, and sometimes they never get out of his department. In some companies less kindly colleagues refer to his department as "the morgue."

On the surface, the bureaucratic boss gives the impression of being a very practical man. Business is business, rules are rules, and what goes for one goes for all. Behind the façade, however, is a little man—rigid, petty, and slavish. There are formalities to be taken care of, and until they are dealt with other things can just wait. Why do things the simple, expeditious way when the department can do them the hard, painstaking way? If the nature of your request happens to fall between two or three bureaucratic bosses in different departments, you can be sure of a merry run-around. It's enough to drive you to the nearest tavern.

Consider this story, recently disclosed by the press: a citizen of an Eastern city—a city in which he was born and reared and which he never left—waited more than a year to get a photostated copy of his birth certificate, which he needed as evidence for admission to a school. Examples of organizational red tape abound. In one bureaucratic organization several employees who were to receive ten-year service pins refused to attend the awards ceremony out of sheer embarrassment. On the scheduled day of the ceremony they had actually been with the company about 13 years! It took a bureaucratic personnel office three years to process the awards. In another company a boss was surprised and amused to see a crew of movers bring into his department several new desks and swivel chairs and a vertical file of drawers. He had put through a requisition for the new equipment two years earlier, had given it up as hopeless after an unpleasant hassle with the purchasing department, and had long since forgotten about it. Now he was in smaller quarters and had little need for all the new furniture.

The visitor to the bureaucrat's department is left numb with the secrecy, the nitpicking, the delay tactics, the suspiciousness, the take-it-or-leave-it attitude, and the frightful formalism. The new employee in the department receives the full baptism, the thorough indoctrination, and is admonished by this boss: "And, now, never let me catch you thinking!"

Tendencies

The most pronounced tendency of the bureaucratic boss is to allow things to get stalled, temporarily shelved, or even killed when they reach his office. This drives many a department head to frustration. Obviously, it leads to another problem: the petty bureaucrat finds himself surrounded by antagonists, some of whom are determined to become freewheelers in order to get around him and his rigid system. An alienation develops between his department and other departments, offices, or units that have to do business with him.

Sooner or later, it becomes evident that the bureaucrat is intent upon means, not ends. Despite his glorification of company objectives, plans, and goals, in his own little monastery he remains consecrated to means—techniques, rules, methods, and procedures. The plant may be due any day now for inspection for renewal of its insurance, but the bureaucrat will not release the data on facilities until there is a supportive request in writing from the safety director. And the safety director and his deputy are both away at a conference in Denver and will not be back for a week. Or a group of employees may have suggested an improvement in factory operations that will reduce the amount of pollutants emitted at the plant. They are anxious to see this suggestion implemented—not only because of the $25 award for each of them but because of the immediate benefits to the company. The boss in charge of reviewing proposals under the formal suggestions-systems program insists that all suggestions are to be reviewed in turn on the basis of the dates submitted. Chronology, rather than purpose, is to prevail. So the suggestion takes its place in a stack and remains there until its day is due.

The way in which the bureaucrat manages the department inevitably reduces the work of subordinates to routine and generally dull tasks. Subordinates become demoralized, for their jobs lack interest and challenge. Once they have learned the ropes, they too answer with a flat yes or no, leaving no opening for further consideration, other options, or exceptions to the rule even when warranted. They too take on an attitude of indifference. They find it easy to ape the boss: he takes no risks, so neither will they.

Another characteristic of the bureaucrat is his tendency to provoke conflict. This is a serious matter, especially when the question revolves around policy. Very often his adamant "Don't blame me; it's company policy, and I don't make the policies around here" is just a dodge. In many instances, what is now policy became policy because he drafted the recommendation and used all his influence and persuasion to get it accepted. Once it has been codified into policy and made part of the rule-book, he feigns innocence. He is unable to explain its restrictiveness or even its unworkability.

When he is in a staff position—as an administrative assistant, an "assistant to," a staff specialist, or other adviser—the bureaucrat tends to arouse or even intensify conflicts between line and staff. Life is difficult enough between those in staff roles and those in charge of operating line departments. The bureaucrat compounds the problem by retreating to petty measures that prevent a line department from doing what needs to be done. And if he should be overruled in a line and staff dispute, he can become a little tyrant, determined to get even with those who defy him. He carries on a crusade against his adversaries.

He emerges from all this, indeed, as a little man.

Analysis

How do we explain the bureaucratic boss as a dead-ender? There are worshippers, and he is one of them—a very orthodox one. The worshipper in a business organization finds comfort in being a follower. He gains a sense of dedication from his role, and he can do so on faith alone, without good works. One view holds that the petty bureaucrat is a power seeker: he seeks not too much power, just enough to wield it menacingly and to make known his presence. He derives his power by citing the gospel and by standing on the expertise he possesses in his field. You will find this combination whether he is attached to legal counsel, wage and salary administration, procurement, quality control, computer programming, or any other function in the company.

Another view holds that the petty bureaucrat is motivated by revenge. At one time a first-rate technician in his special field, he rose to some extent and then was never able to broaden beyond. At that point he could not progress further in the company. In his disillusionment and bitterness, he retaliates by trying to block the progress of others. The little empire he directs is well equipped with the tools by which he can say no and prove his point by citing the right chapter and verse from the book. Consciously or not, he has now made this a way of life.

Still another theory explains the behavior of this dead-ender in terms of his insecurity. In an effort to compensate for his insecure feelings, he indulges in a good deal of overprotectiveness: he insists on following prescribed rules and procedures, on obtaining multiple approvals and clearances, on taking little or no risks, and on cutting communications to a minimum. In all this, he uses the protective armor of executive directives, policy statements, special bulletins, and administrative manuals to back him up.

Sometimes the heavy hand of tradition in a company can distort the boss's viewpoint and his behavior. Some analysts believe that dead-enders such as the bureaucrat are bred in organizational corpulence. The sheer size and complexity of a large organization could lead to organizational flabbiness, and hidden among the layers of fat are many little bureaucratic pockets. Yet this view is not entirely satisfactory, for the bureaucrat is found in very small organizations as well. Thus the treasurer in a small enterprise, a senior secretary, or even an old-timer foreman could be a formidable bureaucratic hurdle.

Finally, to explain his behavior is to explain his concept of managing. The bureaucrat views his job as bossism in its pocket-sized sense, not as managing in its larger sense. His thing is bossing a little function in his own little way. In office management and other areas this function is often described as management by clerkship. But what and whom does the bureaucrat lead? James Hayes, a perceptive and witty management educator, described such a boss in these terms: "If he has built a department of pipsqueaks, then he is nothing more than the chief pipsqueak."

Let's try to gain some perspective on the petty bureaucrat. For many organizations, this dead-ender is not yet dead—at least not in terms of the need for a control point. True, the petty bureaucrat needs the company. The company, however, also needs him. An organization must have its monitors to assure that policies, procedures, systems, and rules are followed—until such time as these prove ill-conceived or unworkable and need to be revised or scrapped. There would be near anarchy without the monitorship that he performs. In addition, the company needs interpreters—those with technical expertise to interpret and apply the policies and rules. Otherwise, decisions made at higher levels would be ineffectual. A decision is not really a decision until it is carried out.

The organization also needs people to mind the store while others are dashing around making forecasts, presenting plans, attending conferences, formulating programs, and sizing up the marketplace. The bureaucrat minds the store. The problem is that in many instances he minds it too well. A good bird dog has his place in the organization. Pointer or setter, he is needed to search out those actions that might be in violation of established procedures or regulations. Compliance is often necessary in an organization, as is creativity or leadership. So the bureaucrat stands guard to assure, at least in his domain, that there will be compliance. Indeed, Max Weber, one of the first social scientists to study the nature of organizations, maintained that bureaucracy is the most efficient form of organization in that it provides the rule of rationality as against the rule of whim.

How to Work With and Help This Boss

A few don'ts in working with the bureaucratic boss:

☐ Don't shake his faith in the institution. This is the anchor that keeps him from straying further. It gives him some measure of security and protection, and even some peace of mind.

☐ Don't demean his role as a watchdog. Trespassers may try to break in. The company needs someone to stand guard.

☐ Don't be intimidated by his caution. The bureaucratic boss fears that anything you do will set a precedent, and that once a precedent is set the floodgates will be wide open to requests for waivers, exceptions, and deviations from the rulebook. It is a fundamental error in logic. Don't fall for the trap.

☐ Don't let your own expertise (which, after a while, will probably be equal to or better than his) get rusty. Use it productively.

☐ Don't settle for the drudgery and boredom of routine. Something better beyond routine *can* be introduced, if you and your co-workers in the department have the will to do so.

Here are several positive guidelines in handling the bureaucrat:

☐ Get across to him the difference between protectiveness and overprotectiveness, control and overcontrol. Be brazen enough now and then, in your responsibility for reviewing and approving some request, to make a judgment that is liberal or even overgenerous — but still sound and defensible. As the outcome proves to be favorable, show your boss how this necessary piece of business was transacted with promptness, how the department concerned was pleased to be able to proceed with the next step, how your department received a pat on the back for expeditious handling of the matter, and how indeed everybody gained from the cooperation. As evidence accumulates from a sufficient number of such cases, initiated by you and other subordinates, he may in time see that the function he represents is well protected without having to be overprotected.

☐ Grind away at the affliction known as "allness" — the view that everything is either all right or all wrong, all good or all bad, all faithful or all heretic, all yes or all no. This is one of the bureaucrat's ailments. As cases present themselves, try to show him that different situations have to be seen differently and judged on their own merit. Some can be decided in absolute terms; others can be resolved only by making exceptions, modifications, or provisos. Break the insidious pattern of allness.

☐ At an opportune time sit down with your boss and review with him just what the department has accomplished in the past year. The chances are that you and he will be unable to point to anything really distinctive, innovative, or significant. There may not be much to show for a year's work except a repeat of the same old routine. Let it sink in. It may leave him with that gnawing question: Why?

☐ Bring him out of his monastery into the world of reality. Rules, directives, and policies often outlive their usefulness or practicableness. They do not remain dogma forever. Get this point across to him. Despite the wisdom of the Founding Fathers, the Constitution of the United States has had to be amended 25 times. Just as there are changes in corporate systems and objectives, and in the availability of information, technology, and decision-making tools, so there must necessarily be changes in the codified rules that guide the internal workings of the company.

Even the petty bureaucrat doesn't want to be shown up as old-hat, behind the times, or unrealistic. To sustain power, he has to sustain a credible image. Facing up to the world of reality in business, especially in a competitive business, will give him a more credible image without diminishing his authority.

☐ Do all you can to memorize the rulebook, modify it, and even kick it aside if necessary. There are times when the rulebook should be cast aside—for example, when it inhibits actions that are neither harmful, risky, nor undesirable. Protecting the rulebook is not as important as protecting the company.

☐ Convince him that the decisions he makes do not rest in the department. They become a subject of conversation elsewhere. People who are unhappy with a decision that they regard as unilateral or restrictive will gripe about it, and they will find an audience with similar experiences and gripes. Bad news gets around, and the bureaucrat and his department become a target for unfavorable criticism.

A boss such as a bureaucrat can probably force a decision through by citing the rulebook. However, in the long run he cannot make others participate willingly in implementing the decision if it is impractical. Word gets around.

☐ Find a basis by which to protest the burdensome paperwork. The bureaucrat's office is usually deluged with paper, mostly defensive paper. Point out how much of the paperwork is of the department's own doing—because of the pettiness, the insistence upon exchange of written communications, the nitpicking, and the constant need to justify taking action. There are many activities more inspiring than paperwork. As he becomes convinced that the mounting paper load is caused by his overprotectiveness, he may in time reduce both the volume of paper and the extent of his pettiness.

☐ Demolish his notion of winners and losers. A man who can cite the rulebook is not a winner. He is simply a sleuth. The company is not in the business of winners and losers, good guys and bad guys. Counsel with him about his differences with other department heads, line or staff. Stress the importance of breaking down the walls between departments and bring home the point that everyone must work together.

This guideline may be difficult to pursue, since it should really come from top management, not from you. It is top management's job to hammer away at the team concept, to stress that bosses *have* to work together despite their occasional differences. Yet as a subordinate concerned with the well-being and the image of your department, you may at times be in a position to counsel with your boss on the problem of interoffice conflicts and how they can be curtailed.

☐ Treat visitors to your department (or their memos and other communications) with respect. Outsiders do not appreciate being viewed with suspicion, and they resent snide bureaucratic responses. The work of their department is as important as that of your department. Behind their visits or requests is a real concern for plans, commitments, targets, and goals, and they do not appreciate having all this dismissed with a pontifical "No."

☐ Be a yes-man to the bureaucratic boss during your early period of employment in the department. Once you have learned the ropes well and have become competent at your job, use your judgment in agreeing with him. It will bring more satisfaction to your daily job and will improve relationships with other departments.

☐ Encourage him to reexamine his own job and some of its problems. The bureaucrat will argue that his job is what it is because the organization has so decreed it. Here again he is speaking as a member of the corporate priesthood. The fact is that there are several parts to a manager's job: the part that is indeed dictated by the organization; the part that grows out of the very nature of the job (dealing with customers, inspection, intensive research, and so on); and the part that is made by the man. Very often, the manager's own influence on shaping his job tends to be a self-inflicted wound. Only by periodic reexamination can your boss begin to see the picture more clearly and learn that it is possible to modify his job by modifying his behavior.

It is clear that the very core of your effort in helping this boss, the bureaucrat, lies in assisting him to move in two directions: from rigidity to flexibility and from a petty, narrow approach to management to a broad-based, results-oriented approach. Perhaps what the bureaucratic boss needs most of all is a good dose of irreverence. There is potential in the man, and there is a good possibility that he can begin to make some progress in these directions. He will need a shove. Do the shoving.

The POPO Boss

Passed Over, Put On the Shelf

Background Profile

As one of the dead-enders, the POPO has been variously described, through his shorthand title, as "promising once, presently obsolete"; "passed over, put on the shelf"; and "permanently overlooked, pasturing only." In short, he is tagged by upper management as a failure but is still kept on the payroll with the alleged responsibilities of a boss. Whichever description fits the man, the point is that he has become an obsolescent boss. Mediocre, just passable, so-so, possibly deadwood—these are the references to the POPO and his performance as a manager.

Many a boss has had his Chappaquidick, and your boss may be one of them. The POPO may not be obsolescent at all. He may simply have been written off by the company because of some prior blunder or poor decision, some act of noncooperation, some poor advice that resulted in embarrassment or difficulty for a superior, some personality clash with a colleague or unpleasant run-in with a VIP. Or his problem may be traceable to a merger two years ago or to a reorganization in which his job was splintered and divided among three people, leaving him with virtually no responsibility. In any event, the POPO is now being given the isolation treatment and is boxed in and underutilized. Top management regards him as a minor leaguer and cuts him out of the more active and challenging projects, programs, and conferences.

On the other hand, it could well be that the job has outgrown the man. He is not measuring up to standards of managerial performance. He has mastered his technical specialty, but he performs poorly in managing the function entrusted to him. There are deficiencies in his planning, coordination, control, direction of the department, delegation, decision making, and other responsibilities. Top management views his output as that of a technician rather than a boss. Or his failure could be due to a serious blind spot. Such bosses do have blind spots, whether they involve people, ideas, values, problems, or living realistically with an organization. They are bosses who lack maturity. The POPO could be paying the price for this deficiency.

Nevertheless, the POPO continues to be a fairly dedicated and diligent worker. Unfortunately, what he is working at is peanuts. His activities are limited in scope and in challenge. Despite his status as a boss, he devotes most of his time to trivia — or, to dignify it a bit, let's call it administrivia. Quite often, higher-ups will deliberately overload him with nonsense work or put him on lifeless committees, just to get him out of the line of fire. When that tactic runs out, they will assign him other special projects or assignments with which he can kill time. His memos receive few acknowledgments, his telephone calls go unanswered, his requests for budgetary changes are put in cold storage, and the ideas he voices at meetings are greeted with silence or dismissed because of urgent agenda considerations. He may not have been aware that he was a dead-ender, but there is little doubt about it now. At this point he cannot really size up his job at all, for there is such a wide gap between his responsibilities and his authority. Frustration sets in slowly but surely.

The frustration is eased a bit because he still has friends in the company who offer him refuge. However, while he has their friendship he may not have their respect. Sooner or later this reveals itself. In the past, his job gave him both friendships and active working relationships. The curtailment of the latter — a result of his loss of responsibilities and isolation — hurts deeply. He is usually disappointed and bitter about the turn of events in his career, but he tries not to betray his feelings. His behavior has changed because of the event or incident that brought him to a halt. He is now somewhat insecure, timid, easily discouraged, reluctant to express his views or convictions, and sensitive to talk around him.

Work and more work is the POPO's chief outlet, his means of saving face, and he spends endless hours working at tasks that are relatively unimportant or even futile. Other outlets include a preoccupation with overhauling the department's office records and files; excessive devotion to his role on a committee; intensive study of new notices, reports, and memoranda; desperate make-work to give the appearance of keeping his secretary busy; long-winded social visits during the day; and paper shuffling just to keep in the mainstream of the company's internal communications. The POPO's conversations are filled with references to the good old days and his past accomplishments. Chronic absenteeism begins to show on his record for the first time in years. These symptoms tell only the surface story. Beneath is an emotional churning of anxiety and fear. The POPO is resentful of his non-recognition and loss of status among co-workers. These feelings erupt now and then into some form of hostility. The POPO lives with a great deal of stress, and there is always the problem of just how much stress he can take without cracking up.

Being bypassed has its severe consequences. The POPO finds it difficult to restructure his work habits. He is concerned that his technical skills will become rusty; he is reluctant to take part in any kind of outside training program for fear that in his absence efforts will be made to demean his job. He is distressed and broods over the fact that his skills and abilities are not being utilized. In short, if he had not been deadwood before, the continuing sequence of events will make him deadwood from here on. He is now clearly a casualty, a dead-ender.

Tendencies

The most serious problem the POPO faces is the erosion of his self-confidence. This erosion is generally of such degree as to rob him of the ability to direct the unit, office, or department he is supposed to lead. The loss of self-confidence leads to other difficulties. In order to hold on to whatever little credit or recognition he has, he becomes a nondelegator. Underutilization of those assets he still possesses is an act of short-sightedness on the part of top management, and the company as well as the man suffers. The POPO's knowledge, skills, special abilities, and experience go untapped. Upper management expects little or no productivity from the POPO, and it gets precisely that. His communications are minimal. It even becomes difficult to get information from him, since he is fearful that once a memorandum is released someone will shoot it full of holes.

The POPO's loss of self-confidence sets up a chain reaction that pushes him close to self-defeat. He begins to doubt his remaining capabilities and seriously downgrades himself. He embarks on projects and assignments with extreme caution. Every detail is checked out, every move justified, every resource considered, and every aspect of the planning examined and reexamined. Burdened with doubt and uncertainty, he begins to fear risk, any risk. This overcautiousness and overdefensiveness seriously inhibit his ability to take action. It would be quite easy to discourage him from moving forward.

Next in terms of severity is the POPO's aversion to problem solving. To acknowledge that the department has a problem of any kind is to hint at further incompetency on his part. He will try to sweep a problem under the rug, blame it on others, deal with symptoms rather than causes, or find some stopgap measure until things blow over. Alibi papers begin to flow. The POPO tends either to run away from a problem or to avoid working seriously at a solution if he can get by with some temporary expedient. If and when he does decide to act, it generally proves to be a case of too little, too late.

As a result of his loss of self-confidence and withdrawal from problem solving, the POPO is no longer the man he once was. He is a different person entirely. He seems to have been drained of his physical energy, mental alertness, and moral courage. He is now a man running scared.

It becomes safer and more secure for the POPO to busy himself with details. Consequently, he fails to give enough time and attention to plans, ideas, organizational improvements, and working relationships — and once again he gets severely criticized for his neglect. The vicious cycle continues to be destructive for this boss.

In time the POPO begins to show resistance to ideas and little responsiveness to suggestions. He becomes quite secretive about his own ideas, always keeping alive the hope that he will be able to spring a proposal at the right time, get it accepted, and in this way recoup some of his lost status. Yet he has difficulty in selling his ideas, not because they lack merit but because he no longer has status as a member of the management team.

All these tendencies take their toll on subordinates and on the department as a whole. Like the bureaucrat, the POPO clogs the pipeline and blocks the movement of others. Lowered morale prevails among subordinates because of the department's general lack of leadership and preoccupation with day-to-day details. Squabbles, blame fixing, and irritability rise in the department because of the decline in morale. Subordinates regard the POPO's resistance to change as apathetic management, and they make no effort to offer suggestions. Despite technological advances in the field, changing competition, and corporate concern with new goals, the department continues to do things today as it did them three or four years ago. Subordinates are unhappy with this treadmill. The department gets no recognition, nor do they. In the more serious cases, a considerable degree of distrust develops between the POPO and his subordinates.

He is in a rut. By this time everyone has forgotten whether he got into the rut through his own ineptness or whether he was pushed into it. It is clear that while he is in this rut the department is stalemated. The department is not moving in any direction; it is just idling. Any careless handling of the gears could quickly slip the department in reverse.

Analysis

How do we explain the behavior of the POPO? Fear is the most important factor influencing his behavior on the job. He has been tagged as a failure by management — whatever its fuzzy definition of failure — and now he is obsessed with the fear of more failure. Hence he avoids the risks that come with problem solving and decision making. The less one does, the fewer the risks. And the fewer the risks, the less likely that one will have to face further charges of failure. Unfortunately, the manager who is caught in this trap is also caught in another trap: little risks, little results. And results are the measure of the manager.

Another factor influencing the behavior of the POPO is insecurity, which is inevitably allied with fear. The POPO's insecurity may be derived from his sense of personal limitation, from the series of setbacks he has incurred, from his uncertainty about what management expects of him, from the continuing anxiety that he will be removed and replaced by another man, or from the haunting fear that he will fail again on the next assignment or project.

The POPO's fear and insecurity combine to produce a great deal of stress. The continuing stressful climate on the job takes its toll of this boss. It produces internal conflict, and a man at war with himself does not manage rationally. Ordinarily, some tension is not bad. It stimulates the adrenals, energizes the man to fight, and pulls him out of an occasional state of lethargy. But excessive tension, sustained tension, unresolved tension is bad. In some cases it induces poor attitudes, suspicion, resentment, a desire to retaliate, and possibly hostility. In other cases excessive tension becomes debilitating: it induces mental fatigue, indifference and resignation, minimal effort, avoidance, the search for protective mechanisms, pessimism, gloom, physical distress, and even some form of withdrawal. In extreme cases it leads to paranoia: the POPO becomes obsessed with the idea that enemies are lurking everywhere and they must be eradicated at all costs. Little wonder, then, that a manager can fall apart under the burden of such stress.

Deprived of motivational drive, the POPO often finds himself filled with self-pity and feelings of guilt. This may occur when the POPO reflects upon the big gap between his aspirations and his accomplishments, between what he had hoped for and dreamed of reaching and what he has actually achieved in life. Indulgence in self-pity and guilt compounds the stress and insecurity. It is destructive to direct these feelings inward and potentially destructive to direct them outward as well—toward someone or something that can serve as a target.

Another explanation of the POPO's dilemma is his narrowness. He may be the victim of overspecialization. While a high degree of technical expertise may be his strength, it may also prove to be his downfall. Many a POPO has come to a dead end because of his inability to expand beyond his technical competency and to acquire supervisory or managerial competency. He fails to see that, once put into the position of boss, he is no longer on the payroll for his technical abilities. He is now on the payroll to tap and direct the technical abilities of others and through them to obtain results in his department. It has been observed many times that experience as a technical specialist is essential at the start of a man's career in management. But if exposed too long to this type of experience, the man will be narrowed by it. As Peter Drucker cautions: "He will come to mistake his own corner for the whole building." And so the POPO may be paying the price for his overreliance on technical skills and for his inability to broaden himself as a boss.

To rush forward with the explanation "Aha, there's the Peter Principle—the man who has hit his level of incompetency" is premature and probably unproductive. For there remains the question of whose so-called incompetency is involved. There is always the possibility that part or much of the blame for the POPO's failure lies with the company itself: the company may have failed rather than the man. The company may have pushed him to higher responsibility too fast for his own good, without having given enough thought to matching the man and the job. It may have provided him with only perfunctory training in how to cope with the responsibilities of a boss. Or the company may have failed to counsel with him in the early stages of his job, never leveled with him as to his strengths and weaknesses, or never defined his role and responsibilities clearly. Higher-ups may not have given him the authority he needed to carry out his responsibilities. They may have set unrealistic targets for him to achieve, ignored his urgent needs for additional staffing, or kept him in the dark as to objectives, standards, and criteria for appraising supervisory or managerial performance. What could emerge from such mismanagement of the boss is indeed failure. But *whose* failure, the man's or the company's? It is difficult to undo what has been done, and so the individual is consigned to limbo with a title but no authority.

If we are to gain any real insight into when a boss has hit his level of incompetency, we must first raise some serious questions: What kind of competency are we talking about? Is the demonstration of competency inherent solely in the individual, or are others a party to it? Against what standards is incompetency measured? Are such standards known to the practitioner? As a junior accountant moves up to senior accountant to chief cost accountant to deputy controller to director of finance, he is to be evaluated in terms of *different* competencies, not in terms of an expanding or lessening of his first competency — the ability to develop accounting data. The same is true for the practicing lawyer as he moves up to assistant district attorney and on to a judgeship. Practicing law and administering law involve not only higher competencies but, more important, different sets of competencies. And the company, the institution, or the agency is inevitably a party to the demonstration of the caliber of competency. The Peter Principle has its applicability in some cases, to be sure. But it has questionable applicability in other cases and little or no applicability in still other cases. So don't look for a formula in trying to explain the complex problems of the POPO. Just as the individual can be charged with having reached his level of incompetency, so the company can be charged with corporate incompetency. The determination often rests with the nature of the organization, its history, its concern for selecting, developing, and reinforcing managerial talent, its attitude toward dealing with mistakes, and its reward system.

From all this there remains the critical question: How much can the boss take — how strong is his ego? A man with a strong ego can sustain a reversal and snap back, can retain his perspective and see the difference between what is essential and what is minor in meeting his responsibilities. He can fight off discouragement and pessimism and continue to function reasonably well until he is restored to good grace. He can do battle for what he believes in—especially his belief in himself and his potential contribution to the company. A man with a weak ego will exaggerate his hurt, retreat to safety, blame others, become negative, fall into a rut, and accept defeat as a way of life.

Perhaps we can sum it up this way. Any serious study of managers will show that most bosses have neither a very strong ego nor a very weak ego. The sequence of events and the degree of stress will continue to test them. Most—but not all—POPOs should be viewed as men having limited competency at this point in their career but not as being incompetent; as men who render mediocre performance but not malperformance or totally unacceptable performance; as men with the potential to improve under the right climate and with the right guidance but not as men with no further potential. They are managers who have had their share of hardships and difficulties in proving themselves, but they are not failures.

Before we proceed to the guidelines, it would be well to examine how top management views its corps of supervisors, middle managers, and other bosses. The perspective, at least in more progressive companies, is not one of promotion or nonpromotion but of levels of promotability:

promotable, immediately: a manager who is ready to take on higher responsibilities now.

promotable, deferred: a manager who, with additional experience in selected areas and with more varied responsibilities, will probably be ready for promotion within a year.

marginal, but with potential: a manager who, with exposure to well-selected training programs and increased self-development, could be considered for higher or different responsibilities and even for promotion in two to three years.

nonpromotable: a manager who is incapable of moving up in the organization.

It is evident that there is still hope for the POPO if he is given a shove and a fair opportunity.

How to Work With and Help This Boss

Many a POPO boss can improve his present mediocre performance, broaden himself as a manager, and reconstruct his attitudes and thereby his behavior. You can help him. Hopefully, if there are signs of renewed enthusiasm and improved performance, his superiors may take notice and lend a hand in helping him on the road back.

Several don'ts are in order:

☐ Don't write him off and don't subscribe to upper management's judgment that he is a has-been.

☐ Don't spend time sympathizing with him. What he needs is self-confidence, activity, responsibility, and a taste of decision making again.

☐ Don't do anything that might cause him to regard you as a threat to his job. He has anxieties enough without anticipating an "Et tu, Bruté?" If you really are out to take his job, don't pretend to help him look good.

☐ Don't fall for the trite gossip around to the effect that this is what happens to an oldtimer when he starts to slow down. Take a good look at your boss. You may find that he isn't much older than you. In any event, he may well have some 15 to 20 years to go with the company. Try to empathize with him.

☐ Don't let him settle for outside satisfactions to compensate for his frustrations in the company. He may indeed find relief from stress by spending a weekend in the mountains, redoing the recreation room in his home, visiting his son and daughter-in-law, or serving on the building committee for the local church. Such outlets are obviously good medicine. However, these outside activities are not adequate substitutes for his fundamental needs on the job: for renewed self-esteem, a sense of worth, and a feeling that he is contributing to the company.

☐ Don't try to advise him on how to live with stress and tension — problems that beset many middle-aged men who are pressured and frustrated. He will have to seek the aid of a trained professional, such as a physician, lawyer, clergyman, marriage counselor, or psychologist. Sometimes a close confidant, wise in the ways of people and their problems, could advise well. But you are not qualified to render such advice, so refrain from doing so.

Have empathy for the man and his problems; listen, but do not give off-the-cuff advice on how to live with stress. It is one thing to tell him to take obstacles in stride and to assure him that you and your co-workers will give him a hand. It is quite another thing to get to the deeper roots of his fears and frustrations. He may or may not want to see an adviser, but that is his prerogative. He cannot and should not expect your advice on such problems.

Here are some key guidelines in working with the POPO boss:

☐ Bolster his self-confidence. The best way to do this is to start showing him small but definite achievements in the department. These need not be extraordinary, just tangible and contributory. For example, get the green light to go forward with an experimental project; make a formal presentation of a new improvement that will cut the costs of an operation by 15 percent; update the department manual and ask other departments for their comments on some pertinent sections; introduce a minor work simplification and show some of the favorable results; submit a chart showing a drop in absenteeism, decline in turnover rates, or other improvement in the department; inform the safety committee of an excellent record of zero man-days lost because of accidents during the past two months.

These achievements may be small, but they have a high visibility. As evidence of departmental accomplishment—at least accomplishment beyond the day-to-day routine—accumulates, you should see some spark of restored self-confidence in the POPO. You will have to goad him on to these activities, and you will probably have to put in some overtime and do a good portion of the work yourself. In fact, you and several colleagues may have to beat the drums a bit to make others in the department aware of what is being accomplished and what is going on. This kind of self-confidence building is much more effective than any amount of moralizing and counseling.

☐ Get him on a goal-setting kick. In this way, you will be putting him on the same wavelength as top management, with its emphasis on management by objectives. Moreover, it is the most strategic way to leapfrog day-to-day, routine operations. Make him aware that such goals are not in lieu of essential operations but above and beyond these operations. Encourage him to set goals for the department: not too many or too few; not pie-in-the-sky goals or goals that are ridiculously simple; and especially not defensive goals. Help him to develop goals that are attainable and profitable, and that contribute to the future of the business as well as to the department and its operations. Also, encourage him to focus on subgoals consistent with the company's larger objectives and interests. As the department reaches one subgoal, he may be spurred on with some enthusiasm to tackle the next subgoal. Focus on relatively short-term and perhaps intermediate-term goals— that is, goals with target dates of six months, nine months, or a year or so. Every successful attainment of a goal will have tangible results—something to brag about.

In order to be effective, goal setting must be a joint venture. This means, of course, that you must do more than just encourage your boss to establish goals for the department. You and others must participate in the process: in considering alternate goals, drafting a feasible goal, refining and modifying the chosen goal as necessary, setting out the road map by which the department is to travel, determining the inputs and resources needed, and appraising the results at different stages. Finally, discuss with your boss the importance of abandoning goals if subsequent developments or circumstances prove them to be unfeasible.

One of management's charges against the POPO is that his outlook is incompatible with the company's accent on progress and that therefore he cannot be counted on as one of the active management team. If anything can counteract this charge and prove that he is a member of the team, it is goal setting and goal accomplishment. Indeed, this is the most effective way to persuade top management that he still has a good deal on the ball. Moreover, it will keep the POPO young in ideas. It's been a long time.

☐ Help him to size up his job better and more realistically. The job of the POPO is no different from that of any modern manager. At any given time a boss is expected to strike a balance between short-term results and long-term objectives in his department. The dimensions of a manager's job are these:

Managing day-to-day operations: keeping on top of things.
Reinforcing relationships: building and improving working relationships upward, laterally, and downward in the organization.
Being problem-oriented: anticipating problems, analyzing them, getting to the real causes, and developing possible solutions.
Being innovative: showing continuing alertness to new approaches, improvements in services, possible organizational changes, and mechanization when feasible; developing plans for new or expanded programs; and making better use of existing resources (people, facilities, space, money, and equipment).

Some bosses are scared of the term "innovation," for it suggests to them a big breakthrough, an invention, a technological change, or some other major event. Don't let your boss, the POPO, be frightened by this term. Explain to him that within your department (or shop, office, plant, or district, etc.) innovation means simply this: thinking of new, different, practical ideas that will make work easier, better, more efficient, or more productive. Innovation in your department can also mean developing ideas which will make jobs more interesting and challenging to employees and which will reduce the number of monotonous, routine tasks they must perform.

One boss was confronted with this sign, framed and prominently displayed on the wall: "Everything now being done is going to be done differently, it's going to be done better; and if you don't do it, your competitor will!"

These, in addition to management by objectives (goals and results), are the main aspects of your boss's job. Help him to size up his job according to these dimensions and to maintain the necessary balance among them — to avoid going overboard on one to the neglect of another.

☐ Persuade him to break away from his forte, his technical expertise. Open his eyes to the fact that this may be one of the things holding him back. Counteract his tendency toward overspecialization. If he is able to size up his job accurately, he will soon realize what should command his time. He will then begin to rely more and more on you and your co-workers for the technical performance of the department.

He may be concerned as to what this will leave him in the way of technical or functional productivity. The answer is apparent. His role should be this: to impart his knowledge and experience to his subordinates; to keep abreast of the latest advances or developments in the field and to pass them on to his people; to review their technical output as necessary; to be aware of who is making technical or production errors and why; to help subordinates correct their errors and learn from their mistakes; and to spot-check the work of subordinates to make sure that they are now on the right path. In addition, he should be available to troubleshoot difficult technical problems in the department and to undertake technical work himself now and then if there is some exceptional project that calls for his special knowledge and experience. This is more than enough to allay his fears about how to use the skills he has acquired over the years.

The main point to be gotten across to your boss is that it is possible to multiply himself through his subordinates and at the same time to maintain reasonable control over the volume and quality of work that goes out of his department. This should spring him loose to devote more time to the other important dimensions of his job.

One effective way to broaden the POPO's outlook and to counteract his tendency toward overspecialization is to make him more versatile. There's not much you can do about this, unfortunately. His superiors are the ones to provide him with an opportunity to display his versatility by assigning him special projects and tasks. If he follows the guidelines outlined above and shows some improvement in his performance, his superiors may well give him such an opportunity. However, if he resists these guidelines, he is not only a dead-ender but a dead duck, and top management will write him off forever.

☐ Block his path if he tries to run away from problems. A boss is paid for solving problems and making decisions, and if he defaults in these he is a goner. The POPO's main fear is that because he has been tagged as a failure before, he will fail again and incur the ill will of his superiors. This risk is inescapable, but he need not fear it. There are several things you can do.

First, try to head off a problem in its early stages, before it reaches severe proportions. Get your antennae out to detect any trouble ahead. You can reduce the risk and protect your boss in this way. The problem can be handled more easily and more effectively in its incipient stage.

Second, slowly but surely impress upon him that very often a problem also poses an opportunity: an opportunity to take a fresh look at an operation long taken for granted; an opportunity to see more options than he did in the past; an opportunity to modify or eliminate some obsolescent requirement; an opportunity to deal with causes rather than solely with symptoms; an opportunity to develop more realistic plans rather than settle for stopgap measures; and an opportunity to make a decision that will lick a problem once and for all.

Third, bolster his courage to take risks—rational risks. A boss should not be allowed to believe that he can avoid risk. There is no such thing as riskless management; there is only the intelligent handling of risk. His main concern should be with the quality of analysis of the problem, the ability to identify the right issue, the feasibility and acceptability of the proposed solution, and the timing of his decision. If these are well considered, then risk is at least substantially minimized. But it is never eliminated.

Fourth, be a problem solver with him. This is nothing new to those who endorse participative or consultative management, who emphasize bringing subordinates in on the task of problem solving. There are factors that inhibit the POPO from taking action. He may tend to oversimplify the problem. It is a common error of his to see only part of the problem rather than the whole. Don't let him get away with it. Cite other aspects of the problem that he may have overlooked: questions of logistics, financing, morale, scheduling, and so on.

On the other hand, the POPO may tend to overcomplicate a problem. Bring him back to reality. Indicate that he is being asked to make a decision only on the problem at hand and not on the entire program. For example, he may be an assistant director of personnel faced with the problem of hiring trainees for the summer period, young people who will be going back to college in the fall. Get him to concentrate on the criteria for selecting them, the kind of work they can do productively for two months or so, and the advantages to be gained by trying to persuade them to join the company as full-time employees after graduation. Don't let him magnify the problem into one of manpower forecasting and planning, adaptation of salary scales, temporary versus permanent employees, union versus nonunion status, and other elements of the personnel program. Work with your boss, then, to see that he neither oversimplifies nor overcomplicates problems.

He may also tend to regard a problem as "the same old thing back with us again." Get him to understand that problems are not static; they change. They change in the number of people they affect, in their scope and complexity, in the type of information they depend upon, in their legal ramifications, and so on. It may not be the same old problem at all.

As a subordinate and as a friend, let him know if *he* is part of the problem. You will not be doing him a favor by withholding the fact that his own misjudgment, inaccurate information, or hasty assumption either caused or intensified the problem. If you don't level with him, you are inviting a repeat of the situation. Do it discreetly and privately, but do it. If he is a party to the problem, he must be alerted to the fact.

Finally, prod him into making a decision rather than just sitting on it. Timing is important in facing up to a problem. A decision that has lost its timeliness has lost its impact. So if he is indecisive, reassure him that he has probed the problem sufficiently and has selected the best possible course of action. Then urge him to get it on its way. Keep needling and goading him. If he continues to stall, you may have to let him pay the price for his indecisiveness — the price of sharp criticism from his superiors. Perhaps he will learn the importance of the element of timing.

☐ Let others know that your boss is on the road to a comeback. Spread the word strategically when and where you can and support it with some tangible example of accomplishment or change. Quietly and discreetly, let the word get around that the department is not willing to accept the verdict that its boss is a dead-ender.

☐ Discourage him from trying to live in the image of his predecessor, especially if his predecessor is still with the company. He will have to be his own man and do his own thing — with your help.

Special Focus

The problem of saving face, one of the POPO's major concerns, needs to be examined further. A manager will experience loss of face when he fails to perform well or falls short of what is expected of him in the way of results. The severity of the loss depends not only on his temperament or strength but also on the context in which the incident occurs, the sense of security he feels with his boss and his co-workers, and other factors.

It is important to distinguish between saving face and restoring face. Saving face is generally a matter of tactics, impromptu or planned, for salvaging all or part of a person's self-esteem. It is an effort to cover embarrassment in the eyes of others.

Restoring face is not a tactic but a process of reconstruction. It is an effort to bring about a healthy psychological balance in someone who has been too long harassed with fear, anxieties, and tension. The process of restoring face involves more action on the part of the man himself — a willingness to evaluate himself, his behavior, and his outlook. It means facing the facts of competitive life, holding to professional standards, being able to take a beating and then snap back to carry on, taking criticism constructively, and cutting a path that will lead him back to self-respect and achievement.

Your role with the POPO boss is to help him restore face. Don't let him accept being written off as a dead-ender unless he definitely is—and knows he is—incompetent. He should not be willing to accept defeat too readily at the age of 35, 40, or 50 in the business world. There is still a long way to go. And while he is making his comeback, give him a copy of John Gardner's book *Self-Renewal.*[1]

The late Dr. Morris Adler, a wise and distinguished religious leader, probably had the POPO boss in mind when he counseled: "God does not despair of man, so man need not despair of himself."

---

[1] John W. Gardner, *Self-Renewal* (New York: Harper & Row, 1963).

The Menopausal Boss

The Lame Duck Years

Background Profile

We move on to the last of the dead-enders—the menopausal boss. Various labels have been used to describe this dead-ender and his tenure with the company: lame duck, pasturing until retirement, spinner of tales, the bonus years.

Whatever the label given this boss, his behavior is distressing to those who work with him every day. Superiors, co-workers, and subordinates wonder how long the company can take it. His management of the department can be described as infertile, ungenerative. It has been a long time since he has shown any ability to originate ideas or to embark on something new for his department. The mental ovulation is gone. So are the warmth and glow of the job. Apathy has set in and management has become drudgery.

The petty bureaucrat and the POPO often know they are dead-enders and sometimes they even know why. The menopausal boss generally doesn't know he is a dead-ender. He thinks of his current position in the company as just a change of pace, and his comment betrays it: "I may not have the fire I once had, but I still have the know-how and that's what counts." In all probability the know-how is gone as well as the fire, but nobody has told him so. What he does have—and what does count—are buddies, friends. Management by crony displaces management by objectives.

115

THE MENOPAUSAL BOSS

Deep down, however, he probably does know that it is more than just a change of pace and that the company has written him off as a has-been. He even begins to relish a bit of gossip and rumor—something to divert him. In his off moments and when he is talkative, he will reflect on how nice it is to be "just coasting" after all those years of arduous work and travel. Now let the others take the pressure. These moments of reflection are just interludes. More often he is tense, worried, easily annoyed. It doesn't take much to cause him to be ruffled: an employee checking in 15 minutes late, a minor complaint, a typewriter in need of repair and a delay in the secretarial work, no word on his request for a new parking place, the disappearance of a safety trends chart, or some other incident. Those around him chalk it up to nervousness. He feels it to be more than nervousness but doesn't know precisely what it is.

This boss displays that "tired feeling." Although he will joke about it, those close to him sense his loss of energy, note his difficulty in concentrating, and hear his occasional complaints of back pains. Those who lunch with him regularly find him to be a worrywart. The anxiety is showing through. For all this, however, he is still generally sociable and approachable, and he carries himself well in bearing and in manner. He undergoes some of the same stress as does the POPO, but he has mellowed and learned to live with it.

The foregoing profile is that of a menopausal boss who has been able to control his behavior to some extent and to maintain his poise. There is another type of menopausal boss, however, and his profile shows a much more severe behavior pattern: days of agitation followed by days of depression. This boss is unable to conceal his mental and physical distress. There is a churning of discontent within him that becomes evident in his daily behavior on the job. He is easily angered and will direct his anger at anyone who happens to be nearby. In his telephone conversations he is loud, repetitious, and constantly on the defensive. Any bad news shakes him for most of the day. If one of his subordinates confers with someone outside the department without his approval, he goes into a rage. Discussing a problem with him becomes fruitless after a while because of his obstinacy. He

116

will insist upon a particular point, however inaccurate or inconsequential it may be, and will doggedly pursue it.

If anything goes wrong at the work site, he is quick to pin the blame on others. Should there be any hint that he had a hand in it, he becomes adamant and threatening. Further discussion becomes difficult because his memory is not as sharp as it used to be.

When his mood is not one of agitation, it shifts to one of depression. Those working with him are witness to the many days he is downcast, in the doldrums. On these days his spirits are low and his behavior is marked by moping and brooding. His daily activity consists of eating lunch, bending paper clips, and processing a few selected pieces in his in-basket. Co-workers have come to expect these days, and they keep their distance when he "has the blues."

This boss, then, displays a much more severe behavior pattern than the menopausal boss described earlier. Not only has he ceased to function as a manager; he also finds it increasingly difficult to maintain day-to-day working relationships with others.

Tendencies

The most serious tendency of the menopausal boss is his reluctance or inability to act. With his loss of drive and enthusiasm, both he and the department become stalemated; only that which is required moves. He offers many alibis for holding things in abeyance. Sluggishness characterizes the department as a whole and indifference becomes the dominant mood.

The menopausal boss links himself to tradition and counts on ultraconservatism as his anchor. It's just too late in life to get excited about improving the department's operations. Employees have stopped counting the number of ideas and suggestions he has rejected. He not only shelves ideas; he destroys them. To him, any proposal or suggestion implies a weakness in his department and a criticism of his leadership. What is new is suspect and dangerous. Consequently, he is reluctant to introduce any changes, no matter how promising. He rationalizes his action in a practical way: changes require thought, energy, time, dialogue, and persuasion of others—and that is just too taxing.

Like the POPO and the petty bureaucrat, the menopausal boss breeds stagnation among others. Apathy and indifference spread in his department. Subordinates are held down, and their abilities and skills begin to go stale. They are demoralized by being kept at routine, play-it-safe activities. The result is inevitably minimal productivity in the department, loss of competent employees, or both. Subordinates see no point in waiting for the boss's retirement or demise, and they find other companies in which to practice their craft or profession.

He tends to transfer his disappointment with himself on the company. The company is to blame for his plight. It has not appreciated his years of dedicated service; top management has given him a raw deal in bypassing him several times for promotion. The company is foolish to invest in computers and other new-fangled tools when it has human brainpower available to do things with less error and with better judgment. The small print in the company's pension plan makes it impossible for him to retire without incurring a large financial loss. All this he keeps to himself or expresses cautiously to confidants. The indulgence in self-pity and the search for a target at which to direct his frustration stem from the disappointment of unfulfilled hopes and aspirations.

Within his department communication, the bloodstream of any organization, is sluggish and unhealthy. He views visitors, correspondence, and reports with suspicion; he engages in only the most casual conversations with subordinates. Meetings and conferences are held to a minimum. Consulting with others is regarded as a chore, a nuisance, even a boobytrap. He communicates only to comply with what is required. Despite his complaints about how the company "did him wrong," he reasons that this is a time to conform, to play it safe. Any defiance on his part could strip him of the little dignity he has left as a boss. The flow of even ordinary communications is impaired because of his suspicions, nitpicking, filtering, and even distortion; his behavior at staff meetings is no better. His ability to solve problems and make decisions is at a low ebb and will continue to be.

To obtain relief from the stress he feels on the job, the menopausal boss resorts to two tactics: faking it and buddyism. He has stopped being a boss, but he still goes through the motions. Although stagnation pervades his department and its activities, he is still artful in conveying the impression that the department is being managed. It is amazing how he can keep up the facade from 9:00 A.M. to 5:00 P.M. He has devised many techniques for keeping busy, and his secretary or his heir apparent is usually his chief accomplice.

The friendships he still enjoys in the company offer him solace. Without them, his frustrations and fears would be difficult to bear. Friends go to bat for him and cover up for him whenever they can. Get-togethers with other oldtimers provide him with an outlet for his frustrations: he can gripe about the company and feel secure that his complaints will go no further. Stories, yarns, and recollections bring back memories of better years, of hard work and deserved recognition. This buddyism yields a good feeling not only for the menopausal boss but for other oldtimers as well — the feeling that they are untouchable because they have been around for a long time and still wield authority and power in the company. This is part of the tribalism of the informal organization, and the menopausal boss finds it protective.

Analysis

How do we explain the failure of the menopausal boss? The temptation to jump at simple explanations is strong. Should we dismiss his behavior as an example of the "over-50 syndrome" in business and industry? Should we add him to the list of those who have reached their level of incompetency? Should we shrug him off with an "Oh, well, there are those who make it and those who fail"? Or, in compassion for the man, should we fix the blame on the company for not having interceded long ago in his behalf? These are valid questions, but they do not address themselves to the complexity of the problem of the menopausal boss.

There is some explanation to be found in the process of aging and its resultant problems. The problems associated with aging, even short of senility and other geriatric disorders, have been examined in depth in many books. Indeed, they are a subject worthy of continuing research by highly qualified specialists. But some analysis is within our reach.

Perhaps the most significant explanation of the menopausal boss's behavior is frustration — the frustration a man encounters when he looks back on life and sees a gap between what he aspired to and what he has accomplished. When the gap is particularly large, then helplessness, apathy, and resignation set in — or aggression springs from the frustration. In the former case, the menopausal boss becomes indifferent, bored, and cynical. He resents younger managers and at the same time subconsciously wishes that he were young again and had another chance. In the latter case, he becomes irritable, angry, and obstinate. But all these are symptoms, not causes. The causes of his frustration are the bitterness and guilt he feels at not having attained in life what he dreamed of attaining someday.

Personal obsolescence is another possible explanation. Physical decline is often accompanied by psychological decline. Anxiety, stress, indecision, overcaution, suspicion, impatience, loss of memory, and other symptoms may show up with middle age. There may be a cultural explanation tied in with the physical and psychological. If he associates business leadership with characteristics of masculinity and power (which is often the case in our culture), then he will view the curtailment of his managerial responsibilities as a diminution of his masculinity.

Psychologists often speak of "psychological distance" as a factor influencing the middle-aged man who has stopped growing in his career. Distance in this sense refers to one's involvement with people, issues, and tasks. The menopausal boss has balanced and gratifying relationships with his peers, particularly his own group of buddies. But there is considerable distance in his relationships with his superiors and even with his subordinates. He is only remotely involved in plans, issues, problems, and decisions in the company; in fact, he is very much out in the cold in regard to managerial participation. Considerable distance exists too between him and the sources of power and authority. This feeling of psychological distance, of being left out, is followed by a feeling of lack of usefulness or worth. All this is a blow to his self-esteem. So, he resorts to buddyism and to faking it on the job to make up for his lost self-esteem.

Another explanation is to be found in the words of the menopausal boss himself: "It's nice to be just coasting and to let the others take the pressure." This may be his way of saying that he no longer has to or wants to run the race. Retirement is just around the corner, and he really doesn't care how people view his obsolescence. He may be acknowledging withdrawal; "lame ducking" is to be his way of life until retirement.

Whatever the pattern of frustrated behavior—excessive aggression, regression, resignation—one factor stands out boldly: the element of dependency. The menopausal boss depends on his old skills and knowledge to retain his job, on his long-time friendships to maintain a sense of acceptance, and on the preservation of some authority, even if just token authority, to save face. In some cases, he is also dependent on the paternalism of the company to take care of him. All these provide him with some degree of security. The older the man, the more acute the dependencies.

Much of the behavior of the menopausal boss is attributable to the phenomenon of middle age. No man approaches middle age without inner conflict. He encounters conflict biologically, psychologically, and culturally. For many men, middle age is a period of deep discontent. The die is cast for them professionally. As the distinguished psychiatrist Edmund Bergler explains:

> What the middle-aged man does not achieve in his forties he will generally not achieve later. What this "later" means is not clear to him, and to avoid facing the question he lives timelessly; he acts as though the daily routine would cancel the calendar. His middle-age troubles start when his illusion of timelessness is brutally shattered by facts and incidents to which he cannot blind himself.[1]

Specifically, the menopausal boss is blind to the fact that others are getting ahead while he is standing still.

[1] Edmund Bergler, *Revolt of the Middle-Aged Man* (New York: Grosset & Dunlap, 1967), p. 10.

THE MENOPAUSAL BOSS

Finally, we cannot ignore this simple and straightforward explanation: when advancement stops, incentive declines. The nature of advancement need not only be financial reward. It could be promotion, greater prestige, higher responsibility, new or different responsibility in one's present position, or some special authority to direct a project of importance to the company. Lacking the opportunity for advancement, the menopausal boss loses his incentive and in time becomes committed to routine. As Norman Vincent Peale once remarked, his is "the tragedy of treadmill thoughts."

It is a complex picture indeed, so let us not jump at a facile explanation of the behavior of the menopausal boss.

Before we proceed to the guidelines for the menopausal boss, let us pause for a moment to consider his role in the company before his decline. We can see something commendable in his career. He could well point with pride to his many years of dedicated service. He discharged his responsibilities well at other levels and in other positions. His special expertise was often called upon to help the company out of a difficulty. His advice was heeded on many occasions, and it made managerial decisions easier and better. He broke in many newcomers to the staff, some of whom eventually moved to positions of high authority. In perspective, his contributions to the department and to the company have not been meager.

Then came menopause. The body's estrogen supply fell to a low level, so to speak. And in this case there is no equivalent of estrogen replacement therapy. Does the company have an obligation to take care of this boss, to look out for his emotional well-being? This is always a matter of balancing conflicting objectives: corporate conscience must be weighed against what can be done practically to help the dead-ender. Among the measures some companies have taken are the following:

☐ Reassign him to a less significant position, especially one that will keep him out of the line of fire; sometimes this is a demotion.

☐ Counsel with him to see what he feels he can still do to contribute to the company; try to accommodate him if possible.

☐ Transfer him to a plant, office, or unit in another geographic location where he will be less active and have less pressure.

☐ Have a showdown with him and demand that he measure up or else.

☐ Give him the functional bypass—that is, let him retain his title, salary, and symbols of authority but have others take over his responsibilities—either by reorganizing his department or by rewriting his job description.

☐ Designate him as a staff adviser and use him on special projects but do not give him authority over others.

☐ Assign a hatchet man to chop him off the payroll.

☐ Break up the oldtimers' clique.

☐ Work out some acceptable arrangement for early retirement.

☐ Indulge in behind-the-scenes politicking to break his spirit and force him to quit on his own.

☐ Send him to a management seminar for a few days, not so much to retrain him as to see if it might rekindle his interest in and enthusiasm for his job.

☐ Let nature take its course and see if he will voluntarily ask for a change or for retirement.

☐ Dismiss him—usually with some offer to help him locate another job.

It should be noted that some companies are giving more serious thought to this problem. Union Carbide, for example, has made some efforts at retraining, redirection, job engineering, counseling, and setting up more teamwork activities (rather than individual activities) so that the obsolescent manager can contribute his functional expertise.

For the most part, however, business and industry have displayed little corporate conscience in regard to this boss. A company may struggle somewhat because of the man's loyalty to the organization, management's reluctance to incur the ill will of his friends, the fear on the part of higher-ups that someday they too will become victims, and the concern about lessening the blow to his already weakened self-esteem. But in the long run business organizations regard this manager as just another link in the corporate sausage. There is concern, perhaps, but not much humaneness. What is done is determined by what is practicable.

How to Work With and Help This Boss

First, several don'ts in working with the menopausal boss:

☐ Don't knock his link with tradition. Everyone is dependent on tradition to some extent—the menopausal boss only more so. This is one of the crutches on which he must lean.

☐ Don't gossip about his cocktails for two. If he finds relief from stress by going out for a half-hour or so to meet with a friend, this is an escape valve. Do not let it become a source of gossip.

☐ Don't try to make him feel better by citing your own problems or those of a friend. This is not a matter of relativity. You don't solve other people's problems by talking about your own.

☐ Don't wetnurse him.

☐ Don't knock his caution or tact, or even his slowness. These are sometimes assets in a smaller company, just as drive and imagination are assets in a larger company.

☐ Don't envy his faking it on the job. An eight-hour day of hard work and hustle is long enough. An eight-hour day of doing nothing is almost interminable. So don't envy him for taking it easy—and don't let on that you and others know. There's a limit to demoralization.

Among the positive guidelines for handling this dead-ender are the following:

☐ Do his work for him—if you feel that the well-being of the department is at stake. When he shows you a memorandum or an official directive that calls for taking action, strike out on your own and draft whatever recommendations you can—for plans, programs, budget needs, and so on. Once he feels sure that your recommendations present little or no risk and that they will be well received by top management, the chances are that he will review and approve them. Intervene in his affairs, if you have to, to avoid situations that in your judgment might become troublesome if left unattended.

You are under no obligation to do his work for him, of course. But if you are really concerned about adverse criticism of the department, you might want to do it. If he raps your knuckles for interfering, take it in stride. This is the price for continuing to work with a lame duck boss.

☐ In dealing with that "tired feeling" of his, learn something about his habits, his body chemistry, and his moods. Know the periods when he is most at ease with others and is willing to listen, the times when he finds it difficult to concentrate, the moments when he wants to be alone, and the times when he likes to be active. This is one way in which you can help to relieve his stress.

☐ Shield him from bad publicity, and protect him from those in the company who are trying to give him a hard time.

☐ Bring him back to reality when he talks of retirement being just around the corner—both you and he know that just around the corner means five years or more.

☐ Caution him about the boobytraps he might be stepping into in the course of administering the department, and remind him of its accountability to top management. He may not be thinking clearly, because of the stress he is under most of the time, and emotions often get in the way of good judgment. You can help to straighten him out. Do it discreetly, but don't minimize the boobytraps and their consequences.

☐ Oppose managerial featherbedding. If either he or upper management is thinking of adding a new staff member or coordinator to assist him, do all you can to sabotage the effort. You must oppose it: first, because the new assistant will probably be out to knife him in the back and, second, because there is no real work for an additional assistant. In fact, there isn't even enough work for him.

☐ Reinforce his self-confidence whenever you can. Do it in a genuine way, without false flattery. Seek his advice and expertise and express thanks for it; comment on how valuable his experience and judgment are in a particular situation; offer a word of praise when he moves promptly in getting on top of a problem. In short, build up his self-confidence as often as possible.

☐ Fire him up occasionally by spotlighting a good opportunity that has just come along: point out how the department can create its own opportunity by taking on a more challenging project or more diversified work. Check first to be sure that there is indeed such an opportunity and that nobody will be blocking the way. Let him know that you and your co-workers are eager to mobilize your skills and energies to get the project off to a good start. Involve him in it as much as possible so that he can feel it is his doing as well as yours. Recognizing and taking advantage of opportunities can do more to energize this dead-ender than any amount of counseling.

☐ Emphasize experimentation. Urge him to try out new approaches that are consistent with the work of the department. The menopausal boss will place most of the emphasis on precedent, and on tradition. These are his defenses in making decisions. Reassure him that you and your co-workers respect precedent and tradition in the company, but encourage him to balance these out with new approaches that will enhance the reputation of the department and its contribution to the company. Your task will be easier if you press for new approaches that are consistent with changes anticipated or already taking place in the company. If he gives you the green light, move ahead quickly; but be sure to keep him posted on developments, progress, and problems. Make him feel reasonably secure as you go forward. If there is no budget for the change, fall back on the counsel of the great British physicist Lord Rutherford: "Now that we have no money, we'll have to use our brains."

☐ Try to work with him in setting realistic goals. Goal setting and goal achievement—even if the goals are not extraordinary—sit well with top management. To make him look good, try to persuade him to set realistic and attainable goals for the department.

☐ Try to engage him in work that is meaningful and dignified and that will make him feel he is contributing to the company. This is excellent medicine for the menopausal boss. Keep an eye out for anything that will bring such work his way.

In the long run, every manager must come to terms with physical and psychological changes and with new developments in the business that tax him. A mature manager should have a realistic view of his assets, and he should feel that he is increasing or at least sustaining his contribution to the company. Moreover, a mature manager should in time come to realize that personal goals and corporate goals need not be incompatible. But compatibility can be achieved only if personal or career goals are realistic. To set one's personal goals so high that one can never attain them is to invite career suicide. This kind of thinking, which differentiates the mature manager from the easily frustrated manager in the middle years of life, can only be done by the manager himself. You cannot do it for him.

What you can do is to be a healthy influence on him. Help him to see that there are better ways of handling the stewardship of the department. It will not be easy to make headway on some or even many of these guidelines. You may have difficulty getting through to him. It has been said that managers are like coconuts: they are hard to reach when they are high and hard to get at when they are down. Yet you must try if you want to help this boss and make him look good to *his* boss.

WHEN TO THROW IN THE TOWEL

For all the guidelines and counsel on what you can do to help your boss, you should not expect too high a batting average. Some of your efforts will show surprisingly substantial results; others will show only moderate results; and in a number of cases, unfortunately, there will be no visible changes at all in his managerial behavior. It is, of course, most distressing to see no tangible behavioral change in your boss; after all your time and effort. You are then faced with two questions: Should you knock yourself out any further with this fellow? If he does not go, should you leave the company? Good questions indeed.

As indicated earlier, you shouldn't even attempt to help

your boss if he is a near retiree pasturing out the few remaining years; a neurotic showing manifestations of paranoic, persecutory, or hostile behavior; a nepotist with a broad umbrella of kinfolk in the company to protect him; or an "untouchable," a man who has more power than he should and who can easily make life difficult for you on the job. There may well be others whom you wouldn't attempt to help.

We have established a broad spectrum of bosses who are worthy of our assistance — in building their self-confidence, raising their level of competency, and otherwise making them perform more effectively as managers. However, there remains the question: When do you give up on a boss?

You should consider throwing in the towel on a boss under circumstances such as these:

☐ When he is part of a layer of organizational fat, and sooner or later top management will trim off the fat in a reorganization. (He'll soon be the victim of a weight-watchers' program.)

☐ When he is on rotational assignment or is with the department for a limited tour of duty. (It's just as well to wait it out and see who his successor will be.)

☐ When he cannot overcome his rigidity, blind spots, or hangups, even after he has given it a good try. (The job will outgrow him in due time, and top management will transfer him to some isolated, harmless spot in the organization just to get him out of the line of fire.)

☐ When his boss doesn't really care whether or not he develops and indulges all his weaknesses and blind spots. (They're made for each other.)

☐ When the company is making lots of money and is too busy at the till to be concerned with its weak and inadequate managers. (Face it — if a company has a good, marketable product, it may make money not because of good management but in spite of it.)

☐ When he is well protected by buddies who cover for him in the management-by-crony kind of organization. (Tribalism has been with us from the beginning of time, and its sociological and psychological roots are deep. You would do well not to fight the tribe.)

So much as to when you might as well give up on your boss.

There is the further question, the more serious question, for the subordinate and his future: When should you leave and try your lot with another company? The decision as to whether you should leave because you feel boxed in depends on a number of factors: your age, the eleventh-hour prospects of getting a transfer to another department, the marketability of your skills elsewhere, your financial situation, the state of the labor market, your aspirations, and other considerations. Few of us have a substantial "go to hell" fund—savings accrued precisely for such occasion when we want to tell the company where to go.

If you are in your 20s or 30s, do not be duped into staying on because of the retirement contributions you've made, the Christmas bonus, the vague promise that your boss will be shifted elsewhere in the near future, or the fact that it is only a 20-minute drive from your home to the plant. If you really want something out of life and cannot see yourself on a treadmill in this company, lures such as these should not be enough to hold you there.

The decision as to when—under what circumstances—you should leave seems quite clear. You should seriously consider looking elsewhere when you are convinced that your performance is only marginal or inadequate because of *his* limitations— when his lack of planning, unwillingness to face up to problems or decisions, inability to delegate, and general ineptness leave you little opportunity to show your skills and talents. You should also consider leaving when you feel that your career aspirations and plans are seriously blocked—again, because of his limitations—and you are only marking time in the company when you could be progressing and growing elsewhere through advancement, new responsibilities, or greater specialization.

But before you decide, be sure it is he and not you who is the cause of your frustration, and be sure you have given it enough time and thought to confirm that all efforts to help him have been to little or no avail.

POSTSCRIPT FOR THE BOSS: advice on how to take advice

Advice is part of "intelligence" in a modern business enterprise. It is regarded as an asset, as are data, reports, tests, and other kinds of information. A boss is therefore expected to take it, screen it, filter it, and then use it profitably if he feels it can be used to advantage. There are times when he will reject it, of course, but he should at least be open-minded. After all, companies make it a point to solicit advice and they pay well for it. Idea men are put on the payroll to develop proposals that will improve the business. Management tries cross-fertilization of viewpoints to encourage the input and evaluation of ideas. New blood is taken into the firm to shake up the lethargy of oldtimers.

Troubleshooters are sent out to diagnose ills and to come up with solutions that will restore the company to its full level of productivity. Staff assistants are asked to probe complex problems and to submit recommendations. Other means are utilized, from the elementary suggestion box to the hiring of outside consultants. So getting advice, sifting it, and using it profitably if possible is important in the life of the modern manager.

Giving subordinates an opportunity to render advice is an important motivational goal. Subordinates gain satisfaction from being involved in plans, decisions, operations, and improvements. They appreciate being able to show their stuff by coming forward with sound advice that will aid the department. Their loyalty is strengthened when they are given a chance to help eliminate weaknesses and wastefulness in the company and to protect its interests and reputation. Contribution and participation are closely linked to the motivation of subordinates.

The Kind of Advice That Reaches You

As a boss with key responsibilities, you must be able to recognize the nature of the advice that reaches you. Advice may take various forms. Here are ten broad categories of advice, with some examples of each:

Admonition: caution—trouble ahead; head it off; expedite action now.

Guidance: look ahead; delay action; think of this outcome; consider this strategy; this might be a wise course to take in moving toward the problem.

Interpretation: this is what it means; it may not be legal; it's policy-safe; let's get clarification; compliance is optional under certain conditions.

Reinforcement: it's been validated; this is precisely the time to go forward with it; we have more ammunition if this runs out; we've got a sound case.

Disagreement: let's modify the proposal; we should drop it entirely; it's contrary to policy; it may jeopardize other aspects of our plans if it fails.

Exhortation: face up to it; we've taken all the guff we should; don't let them get away with it.

Perspective: the problem changes if you look at it this way; it could be expedited; the risk is not as great as we think; here's a different viewpoint; negotiations may not be necessary at all; we may be cracking a frontier.

Information: here are more facts and figures; these are the latest results; let's look at new trends; the computer rerun shows we're on target.

Reassessment: let's take a hard look at it; we've been using an old approach in cost cutting; it's too early to tell; controls may be too lax; our plans ought to be reexamined; perhaps we're relying too much on the San Francisco office.

Tactics: this hole can be plugged; use an extra shift; talk with the union steward first; divide the work between two clerks; tighten up.

This is the sweep of advice that can reach you, the business manager. At any given time, any one of these kinds of advice can be a valuable tool in serving your ends. The important thing is to be able to recognize the nature of the advice you're getting—the pitch that is being made, the purpose, the central theme. It may range from cautious examination ("We don't have enough to go on, sir") to a proposal for brinkmanship ("Let's go for broke on this one"). The strength of conviction behind the advice will vary too. One man will respond with a "Yes, by all means" because he feels you like to be agreed with. Another will propose a show-down because "Like it or not, the stakes are high, and we had better put our brights on before driving in the dark."

What Constitutes Good Advice

Advice is no different from a machine or a system. It is good only when it works, when it produces or is likely to produce bene-

135

ficial results. The wisdom of the advice is not essential, although a touch of wisdom always helps. The real test is practicality: Will it work?

Perhaps the most significant characteristic of good advice is its being on target. For counsel to be on target in regard to timing, content, and utility, it should be derived from several attributes of the adviser. Here are some of the most important:

The adviser has profited from experience. Advice that is linked to some prior experience and evaluation of that experience is likely to be profitable. This is not to say that a recommendation to disregard prior experience — to damn the past and take off in a new, more imaginative direction — will never be sound. But this is the exception rather than the rule.

The adviser has done his homework well. When the man giving the advice has done a thorough job of staff work, the prospects are good that the advice will be sound. Digging into background and unusual circumstances, reviewing records and other relevant data, checking and confirming new facts relative to the current situation — all these are part of the homework a man must do before coming to the boss with advice. Unless advice carries this attribute, it is likely to be poorly thought out, superficial, and off target.

The adviser is an expert. Technical expertise should be built into advice when the nature of the problem calls for it. A boss should expect technical expertise germane to the subject. He should look for it in an evaluation of comparative systems, an analysis of trends, an assessment of recent innovations in the field, and other specific areas.

The advice is timely. Good advice shows sensitivity to the time element. When timing is essential in a given situation, good advice conveys an awareness of the immediacy of the problem; it demonstrates a concern for priorities. When the matter at hand is less pressing, sound advice carries with it a realistic timetable, an evaluation of what and how things are to be accomplished in the short run and in the long run. Just as decisions may be good or bad depending on their timing, so advice on making a decision may be good or bad depending on its sensitivity to time.

The advice has perspective. Good advice enables the boss to see the degree of risk involved in pursuing a particular course of action. It assesses the impact of one function upon another if that course of action is taken, insists on a broader outlook to offset any narrowly conceived proposals, recognizes the administrative support needed in the way of money and manpower, and takes into account the kind of precedent that might be set. Good advice adds depth and logic to the analysis of a problem.

These are some of the most important attributes of good advice. Indeed, they are key criteria for determining the acceptability of advice. As the boss, be sure to search for any unconfirmed facts, inaccurate data, biases, or ulterior motives in the advice that you receive. The testing of the advice is then entirely up to you.

When to Shun Advice

Some clues about when to avoid advice have already been given. Shun advice that is twisted, biased, unconfirmed, poorly timed, or unclear as to the pros and cons. Shun advice that seems to be one-sided, parochial, too technically oriented, or superficial. Avoid advice that overwhelms you with data but lacks interpretation of what all the data mean in the way of trends; advice that armtwists you for action now when the problem isn't important; and advice that smacks of avoidance of risk at any price, and of perpetuating the status quo. Above all, refrain from accepting advice from subordinates because you happen to like them personally. You are, after all, responsible for dealing with the raw material for decisions. Base the decisions on substance and merit, not on sentiment or friendship.

There is a cliché in management: "The boss never makes a mistake; he just gets bad advice." Poor advice can be damaging, of course. As a manager, you must be able to spot the factors that identify advice as unacceptable. In all this, of course, you have to know your people. You should know those who are careful, competent, and exacting in the advice they offer. You should also know those who are not so dependable: the overhaulers, the excessively cautious, the yes-men, the expediters, the overambitious, the nonrealists, the rank-conscious, the theorists, the politicians, and the butter-uppers.

On the other hand, you should not avoid advice simply because it involves controversy or honest differences of opinion. A good part of your responsibility as a manager is to be artful in tolerating differences and in resolving them without stifling those who have strong convictions about what should be done. Nor should you pass up advice just because you have an aversion to people who suggest "sleeping on it" for a day or two. Indeed, deliberating longer may be warranted in any number of cases, and it counteracts the pitfall of moving with too much haste. More time for deliberation and confirmation of facts and trends may be needed. Of course, if delay tactics become evident as the pattern of a man's thinking and appear to be an escapist route, that's another matter.

"Climate" Can Make or Break

You will get much or little in the way of advice depending on the climate of acceptance you encourage. You will get good or shoddy advice depending on the climate. You will get enthusiastic or grudging advice depending on the climate. And it is you, the boss, who creates the climate that prevails in the department. If you have surrounded yourself with competent, productive, and reasonably dedicated subordinates, you have the makings of a solid staff of advisers to assist you in solving the many and varied problems that emerge in your department. This important resource can be tapped if the climate is right. Be approachable.

You can create the right climate in several ways. First, set a good example of consultative management. Show a willingness to see other viewpoints and to tolerate unpopular views; be available to confer and consult with subordinates; give employees your attention and concentration; be communication-minded. If you set the tone, subordinates will in time respond. Second, learn the art of good listening. Hearing is not enough. Listen to words, emotions, ideas, anxieties; grasp the full meaning of what is being communicated before you come to a judgment. Third, don't be afraid of controversy or heated discussion. Chalk it up philosophically to democracy in the business. Man-to-man differences and candor will usually work out well in the long run. However, if the differences or controversies are geared to departmental rivalries or personal vendettas, step in and take over.

Fourth, bring subordinates in on the decision-making process. When subordinates have some involvement in the issue, the give-and-take of ideas, and the consequences, they feel themselves a party to the decision—even though that decision is ultimately yours. Knowing what goes into the decision-making process and having an opportunity to see it operate is a great energizer for subordinates. They then become more critical in the quality of assessing the advice they render. Being ancillary to a decision, even though the boss eventually makes the decision, is not false participation. Indeed, it is a valuable tool for getting technical specialists to break out of their shell and to learn how managers face up to decisions and deal with risk.

Finally, give credit where it is due. Hoarding credit and palming off ideas as your own will not raise your stature in the eyes of subordinates. In time, even your bosses will catch up with you; they will know whom you tapped and what you pirated. If good advice leads to a good decision, parcel out enough credit to bring satisfaction to those responsible for it. When a job is well done, the department looks good and you look good; your subordinates who contributed to it should also look good. A pat on the back, a word of commendation, a compliment at the next staff meeting, a special memorandum of recognition to go into the personnel file if warranted—all these are ways of extending credit and recognition when due.

Perhaps a summation of how to seek and give advice can be stated in this way. Let subordinates feel free to seek your advice without feeling foolish or stupid and without having to admit failure. In turn, accept their advice without taking it personally— without feeling that you or the unit you manage is being unduly criticized or attacked.

POSTSCRIPT FOR THE SUBORDINATE: what an effective boss is expected to do

It is astonishing to learn how many subordinates view hustling around, frantic telephone calls, order giving, hurried lunches, and paper shuffling as managing. This is activity, not management.

As a subordinate, you should be aware of the key responsibilities that every manager is expected to discharge. Such an awareness will enable you to know the frame of reference of your own job and its dimensions and responsibilities. And the greater your knowledge the better your chances of being helpful to your boss.

There is no mystique in management. Managing is partially a science—in the sense that some of the body of applied knowledge is derived from industrial engineering, psychology, mathematics, sociology, economics, logic, and other disciplines. Managing is also partially an art—in the sense that a manager has to be artful in attaining balance and in effectively dealing with certain situations in the work environment. The fusion of both is needed as the manager contends with problems and decisions that involve goals, facilities, schedules, programs, services, workloads, people, data, paperwork, and other matters.

The outline below should give you the orientation you need to understand what a manager is expected to do. Obviously, the range of what is expected will vary depending on the level of responsibility of the manager—from supervisor to foreman to superintendent to production manager to executive. The higher the rank, the more he will be involved in forecasting, planning, and policy determination; the lower the rank, the more he will be involved in directing, controlling, and general operational management. This is self-evident. However, the outline provides a useful guide as to what managers are universally expected to do.

A manager is responsible, within his organizational unit, for the following key elements and processes of management:

planning . . . which includes

1. Establishing and interpreting goals and objectives.
2. Formulating and issuing policies that are, in effect, standing management decisions.
3. Establishing programs—functions and activities to be pursued in reaching the goals that have been decided upon and through the guiding policies.
4. Providing the components needed to fulfill the goals and the programs planned—men, money, material, time, facilities, ideas, and other resources necessary for effectively moving ahead.
5. Developing expectations and timetables that are subsequently refined into standards and schedules.
6. Differentiating between short- and long-range plans,

standing plans and interim plans, and other elements of the total planning function.

7. Determining who is to represent the organization in the formulating and revision of plans.

organizing . . . which should provide

1. Alignment of major functions and the proper departmentation and division of organizational structure.
2. Delineation of responsibilities, authority, and accountability of key positions.
3. A sound division of labor and specializations.
4. A system for communicating, coordinating, and reporting.
5. Staffing the people needed to perform management, supervisory, specialization, technical, clerical, maintenance, and other roles.
6. Preparation of manuals, position descriptions, administrative handbooks, and other tools to clarify and make known the responsibilities, authority, and accountability of those to whom functions are assigned.
7. Clarification of delegated authority.
8. Formal and informal organization.
9. Network of relationships—particularly line and staff relationships and headquarters-field relationships.
10. Committees, survey groups, task forces, and other special work units.
11. An organizational framework flexible enough to be changed in periods of stress or growth.

coordinating . . . which focuses on collaboration, integration, and compatibility and attempts to achieve

1. Balance in the set of relationships established.
2. Communication channels in order to check and verify facts or to obtain clearance and authorization.

3. Systematic means for bringing the organization's resources and functional specializations into an integrated whole.
4. Exchange of views, ideas, information, better understanding, plans.
5. Appropriate review and consultation.

motivating . . . which involves

1. Understanding what makes people tick in an enterprise— motivation.
2. Alertness to people's basic and special needs and interests —needs which, if fulfilled to a considerable extent, lead to job satisfaction.
3. Ability to gauge evidences of dissatisfaction that lead to grievances, complaints, absenteeism, poor communication, turnover, and other problems.
4. Providing structure, processes, and participation opportunities conducive to good employee morale.
5. Incentives—and the assessment of their effectiveness.
6. Individual productivity.
7. Intelligent selection and placement of subordinates and a sound compensation system.
8. Means of recognition and reward.
9. Counseling, appraising, coaching, and training subordinates.

directing . . . which is featured by *organizing* plus

1. Installing, launching, and implementing the programs that have been established.
2. Operating the programs, through systems, procedures, processes, and other means designed for them.
3. Making adjustments in staffing, as necessary or desirable.
4. Developing rules, regulations, requirements, and guidelines for effective operations.

5. Supervising operations to assure full utilization of people, money, materials, facilities, and other resources—with a minimum of waste and with concern for high-quality and high-quantity performance.
6. Communicating with upper levels of management as necessary to resolve certain problems.
7. Requirements for reporting and other means of accountability.
8. Enforcement of rules and regulations.

controlling . . . which requires

1. Devising performance standards.
2. Establishing quantitative measures for gauging the adequacy of use of resources or performance of functions.
3. Devising systems for determining the extent to which standards are being met and, if not, the extent of deviation from the standards.
4. Recording and evaluating the completed work—review.
5. Serving, in general, as a feedback of information useful to management in taking action to improve the situation.

In the effort to help your boss, you will find the above outline a useful tool. To the extent that you know what is expected of a manager, you are in a better position to influence him. And to the extent that he knows you have this awareness, he may be more inclined to level with you regarding the performance and the future of the department.

Don't be among those naive people who assume that the busy boss is an effective boss; recognize that there is a body of knowledge that forms the substance of the management field. Familiarize yourself with this body of knowledge—learn before you act.

To summarize, it is not so much what bosses are that matters as what they do—and the artfulness of professionalism with which they do it. Your boss is supposed to be reasonably competent in doing the following:

Planning—setting objectives, goals, and priorities.

Problem solving—finding effective and timely solutions to problems.

Decision making—making decisions that are sound and consistent with company policy.

Delegating—allocating projects willingly and ably.

Evaluating and controlling—gauging results and using feedback well.

Dealing with change—anticipating resistance and overcoming it.

Serving as one of the management team—contributing well to the company as a manager.

Developing the organizational climate—creating a flexible, productive work environment.

Tapping the productiveness of his people—motivating and improving the morale of subordinates.

Communicating—directing communication effectively upward, laterally, and downward in the organization.

Resolving differences—dealing with tensions, strains, and controversy.

Managing time—using his own time judiciously and productively.

Dealing in interpersonal relations—working with others productively.

This is not a small order for your boss or any boss, and there are many times when he will need your productive assistance. This is what it is all about.

FINALE

The central theme has been presented. The rationale for you, the subordinate, helping your boss has been established. The profiles of some of the kinds of bosses you may have to work with have been portrayed. Constructive guidelines by which you can move forward with the task of helping your boss have been posed. This is it.

It would be a grievous waste of human resources to write off your boss as a has-been. Just one factor or another may be the only thing that prevents him from becoming a more competent and effective manager—a pro. He could use your advice and assistance in helping himself to get over this hurdle.

FINALE

Most bosses do have the potential to get out of their rut, to overcome their weaknesses, to raise their level of competency, and to move on to a more satisfying and rewarding life on the job. Your boss may be one of them.

In helping your boss so that he will be able to enlarge his competency and take on new, different, or even higher responsibilities, you will have done much more than helped your boss to save his job; you will also have proved yourself a very real asset to the company with which you are associated.